WHY LEADERSHIP SUCKS

SUCKS

Volume 1

Visit Miles online at www.milesanthonysmith.com and follow him on Twitter @Miles_Anthony.

Why Leadership Sucks: Volume One: The Fundamentals of Level 5 Leadership and Servant Leadership

Copyright © 2012, 2018 by Miles Anthony Smith. All rights reserved.

Cover Design: Tugboat Design

Cover Photo: © ifong/Shutterstock.com (used with permission)

Edited by Matthew Wolf

Scripture quotations marked NLT are taken from the *Holy Bible*, New Living Translation, copyright © 1996, 2004, 2007 by Tyndale House Foundation. Used by permission of Tyndale House Publishers, Inc., Carol Stream, Illinois 60188. All rights reserved.

Scripture quotations marked NIV are taken from the Holy Bible, *New International Version,*® *NIV.*® Copyright © 1973, 1978, 1984, 2011 by Biblica, Inc.® Used by permission of Zondervan. All rights reserved worldwide. www.zondervan.com.

Scripture quotations marked ESV are taken from *The Holy Bible*, English Standard Version® (ESV®), copyright © 2001 by Crossway, a publishing ministry of Good News Publishers. Used by permission. All rights reserved.

ISBN 9780988405301

Contents

Acknowledgments

While there are many who have influenced my thinking on leadership, many of whom I reference in this book, there are several people who challenged me to write and publish this book. And most probably have no knowledge of their impact.

The writings of Seth Godin encouraged me to *Poke the Box* and to "ship" this book. Those of Chris Anderson nudged me to use *Free* to more widely disseminate this book, thus helping more leaders grow faster.

Thank you to Evernote, whose note-taking technology helped me start writing this book.

Thank you to Denis Kreft at Imaginasium, Chris Busch at LightQuest Media, and Chris Elliott at Ameriprise for inspiring me to be a better servant leader.

Thank you to Deborah at Tugboat Design for the cover art on this book. If you need any book cover design, please contact Deborah at tugboatdesign.net.

Thank you to my lovely wife Carolyn, who challenges me, holds me accountable, and loves me for who I am, not what I do. To my three children, Josiah, Reagan, and Dominic, thank you for affording me the liberty to be a child at heart.

Thank you to Matthew Wolf, my brilliant editor! You were an extraordinary help in so many ways. I could not have polished this book without your invaluable, herculean effort. If you want Matthew to edit your book or produce an e-book for you, email him for a quote: wolf.matthew.j@gmail.com

Thank you to everyone else with whom I have had or will have the privilege to cross paths; you have all impacted my life in some way that has contributed to this work.

And, last but not least, thank you to Christ without whom I am nothing, even on my best day.

Introduction

It is literally true that you can succeed best and quickest by *helping* others to succeed.

Napoleon Hill

Why does leadership suck? It sucks because real leadership is hard and requires selfless service. It also sucks because the buck stops here, meaning it is ultimately the leader's responsibility to deal with all of the crap. Lastly, it is easier to be too harsh instead of balancing our hard and soft nature. It requires less effort to "lead" (if you can call it that) in the harsh, dictatorial, selfish way that is so prevalent today. The alternative to selfish "leadership" is servant leadership, or Level 5 leadership (I consider these terms to be synonymous). This book points to the practical steps I have found to move toward becoming a Level 5/servant leader. Level 5 leadership is uncomfortable, humbling, self-denying, painful, and counterintuitive; nonetheless, in the long term, it is the only kind of leadership that brings lasting results, genuine happiness, and true self-fulfillment.

Level 5 Leadership

Jim Collins describes Level 5 leadership in his book *Good to Great* as a paradoxical blend of personal humility and professional will (fierce resolve). He goes on to write of the five attributes Level 5 leaders possess:

1. They are self-confident enough to set up their successors for success.
2. They are humble and modest.
3. They have "unwavering resolve."
4. They display a "workmanlike diligence—more plow horse than show horse."
5. They give credit to others for their success and take full responsibility for poor results. They "attribute much of their success to 'good luck' rather than personal greatness."

Collins's empirical research indicates that the top characteristics of Level 5 Leaders are:

1. *Drive for sustained results:* The difference between the Level 5 and other leaders is that they are driven to produce sustainable results for their organizations. The idea is that Level 5 leaders create long-term, sustainable change.
2. *Set up successors for success:* Level 5 leaders are generally more interested in the success of the organization than in their own personal success. They want to leave a lasting legacy of an organization that continues to prosper. They are self-confident enough to hire competent people (they "get the right people on the bus") and delegate.
3. *Modesty:* Level 5 leaders demonstrate compelling humility. They act with quiet, calm determination; they rely on inspired standards, not inspiring charisma, to motivate.
4. *Take responsibility:* Level 5 leaders stand out because they take responsibility when things go wrong. They do not look to blame others when things do not work out as expected. In addition, they

rarely seek credit for things that go right, generally attributing success to other factors.

5. *Organization focus:* The ambition of the Level 5 leader is first and foremost for the organization. Their desire for success for the organization that they lead far outweighs their drive for personal rewards.

Servant Leadership

I believe that the qualities of a Level 5 leader can be summed up in the term *servant leadership.* This concept originates in the teaching of Christ:

> You know that the rulers in this world lord it over their people, and officials flaunt their authority over those under them. But among you it will be different. Whoever wants to be a leader among you must be your servant, and whoever wants to be first among you must become your slave. For even the Son of Man came not to be served but to serve others and to give his life as a ransom for many.

Matthew 20:25-28, NLT

In 1970, Robert K. Greenleaf brought the idea to leadership literature with his book *The Servant as Leader.* Greenleaf explains the term as follows:

> The servant-leader *is* servant first. . . . It begins with the natural feeling that one wants to serve, to serve *first.* Then conscious choice brings one to aspire to lead. That person is sharply different from one who is *leader* first, perhaps because of the need to assuage an unusual power drive or to acquire material possessions. . . . The leader-first and the servant-first are two extreme types.

Between them there are shadings and blends that are part of the infinite variety of human nature.

The difference manifests itself in the care taken by the servant-first to make sure that other people's highest priority needs are being served. The best test, and difficult to administer, is: Do those served grow as persons? Do they, *while being served*, become healthier, wiser, freer, more autonomous, more likely themselves to become servants? *And*, what is the effect on the least privileged in society? Will they benefit or at least not be further deprived?

What's ironic is that in serving others selflessly, elevating their needs in place of our wants, our own self-fulfillment arises as a natural byproduct. Yet when we attempt to "climb the career ladder" by tearing others down to achieve this shallow version of success, a negative sum game ensues, and everyone loses.

Why Another Leadership Book?

My goal in writing this book is to share things I have learned in my journey thus far in hopes of benefiting other leaders and challenging them to "go further faster."[1] I have a decade of management experience and was fortunate enough to have been given the opportunity to lead organizations starting at 25. So although I am a relative youngster, I believe it should be the goal of every leader to be a coach of leaders. It is not as though I've learned it all and don't make any mistakes. Far from it: I plan to make mistakes—and learn something from them—for the rest of my life. I want my candle to burn steadily bright all of my days.

That brings me to another, more personal reason for writing. I genuinely welcome the accountability that publishing this leadership book brings. If those who work closely with me see that I am not living up to the standards in this book, they have the right and duty to respectfully inform me. I hope those closest to me will kindly and gently remind me of the areas where I miss the mark I espouse in this book. This book is first of all a philosophy for me to constantly review and intentionally implement in my life; secondarily, it can serve as a teaching tool for my immediate family, thirdly to my team members that work alongside me, and fourthly to other current or aspiring leaders.

Here's to becoming a Level 5/Servant Leader. With a consistent, persistent commitment to the right kind of learning, anyone can become a better leader. And I am not saying that this book is the only way to become a Level 5 Servant leader, but these are things I have learned along my journey. This book will hopefully give you a lot of ideas for better habits and attitudes. Don't be overwhelmed by the sheer volume of them. I suggest taking a week to practice one concept; then move on to another the next week.

The leadership lessons are divided into four sections. In part 1, I deal broadly with the topic of service, exploring the choices we make whether to serve or not to serve. Part 2 focuses on what it means to serve your organization before serving yourself. Part 3 keys in on humility, which leads to authentic authority and serving without resentment. Finally, part 4 applies these concepts to the real world: getting results in specific situations.

To thank you for purchasing the paperback or ebook version of *Why Leadership Sucks Volume One*, I am giving you my audiobook on a completely complimentary basis! Whoa, wait a cotton-pickin' minute! "Did I hear you right, Miles?" Yes, you did. All I ask in exchange is that you provide your email address... the one you regularly use (not your generic signup email addy). Hey, I spend a ton of my own time and money recording, editing, mastering, and publishing my audiobook on Audible, iTunes, and Amazon, so it's only fair for you to supply me with a real email address, and I'm happy to provide you with the complimentary audiobook in exchange. And it's not an abridged version; it's the entire audiobook.

To get it, go to milesanthonysmith.com/wls2audiobook and use password GIMMEMYWLS2AUDIOBOOK. Go check it out right now. I'll wait for you to come back to the book! You may want the audiobook version to listen to the contents for the first time or to listen again as a refresher later while you're driving, working out, cooking, washing dishes, buying groceries, shoveling snow, mowing the lawn, eating lunch, doing data entry, waiting at a doctor's office, getting a massage, fishing, painting, or wrapping presents... I think you get the idea that an audiobook can be enjoyed while multitasking; something you can't do with a physical book or ebook!

WARNING!

Many of these topics are true a vast majority of the time, but there will always be minor exceptions. So if you find yourself in a situation that might be an exception to the rule, please keep this in mind.

PART 1

To Serve or Not to Serve, That Is the Question

A rider on horseback, many years ago, came upon a squad of soldiers who were trying to move a heavy piece of timber. A corporal stood by, giving lordly orders to "heave." But the piece of timber was a trifle too heavy for the squad.

"Why don't you help them?" asked the quiet man on the horse, addressing the important corporal.

"Me? Why, I'm a corporal, sir!" Dismounting, the stranger carefully took his place with the soldiers.

"Now, all together boys—heave!" he said. And the big piece of timber slid into place. The stranger mounted his horse and addressed the corporal.

"The next time you have a piece of timber for your men to handle, corporal, send for the commander-in-chief."

The horseman was George Washington, the first American president.

1

Prepare to Face Hatred, Discomfort, Vulnerability, Fear, Betrayal, and Peril

If we go into management to earn more, have more power/prestige, and work less, we are either naïve or ignorant. (And let's admit right now that those are *precisely* the reasons most of us go into management.)

Wise leaders accept that some decisions will be unpopular. If you can't handle others' disapproval, then leadership isn't for you. Trying to be everyone's friend is a futile and selfish effort. Most of us want to be liked; as we progress through school, we do things to get others to accept us (with varying levels of success). We try to wear the cool clothes, have a cool car, or take the cool classes. We then carry those bad habits into the workplace; we do things to attain the approval of others, allowing true accountability to wither. Some of us want so desperately to be accepted that we will sacrifice the good of the rest of the organization for our own selfish emotional gain. While it might help in the short-term, the pursuit of approval is a guarantee of long-term failure. Those who don't throw their leadership opportunities away in pursuit of approval will be teased at best; at worst, they will be ridiculed, mocked, and defamed. So prepare to be hated, but remember that the haters are the ones who don't matter. The ones who do matter will sincerely appreciate your leadership and

3

implicitly trust your guidance, since you have proven your constancy and trustworthiness.

> Staying vulnerable is a risk we have to take if we want to experience connection.

Brené Brown

In life, but especially in leadership positions, we all face fears. We fear not being accepted, feelings of inadequacy, shame, rejection, discomfort, and the list goes on. My response (and I am speaking to myself more loudly than others) is, "We're all afraid . . . so what!" We must choose to get over our fears and not allow them to hinder our growth and development as leaders. So what if we don't have it all together. So what if we didn't go to the right school; so what if we didn't have a good mentor. We all have something to offer, and we must choose to focus on what we do have to offer, not what we don't. And remember the dirty little secret is that those who are acting like they have it all together really don't.

One thing that fuels fears about the future is past betrayals, and betrayal is one of the ultimate tests of leadership. Are we willing to walk in forgiveness with those who betray or seem to have betrayed us? Are we going to wall ourselves off from future close relationships with others, or are we going to allow intimate relationships with others that ultimately might mean another betrayal? I do recommend that we are wise in this, not allowing obviously dysfunctional people close to us, but we can't use that as an excuse to not be vulnerable. I admit that forgiving betrayal is difficult for me, but I must choose to let those circumstances go, since unforgiveness only hurts me, not the other person. I would rather choose to remain vulnerable and be taken advantage of than be so skeptical of others that I have no intimate friendships.

Leaders also get to be uncomfortable; it's part of the job description. At one point, I resigned from a position with a company and had the choice to leave without talking to anyone or come back the next day and give my leaders some closure. As painful and emotional as I knew it would be, I chose the latter and am glad I did. As leaders, we don't have the luxury of shirking painful responsibilities even though we would like to. Leadership is not necessarily safe but can be perilous to our career; it involves much more risk than just being a team member. Our actions as leaders are held to a much higher standard, and criticism of our leadership decisions is much more out in the open for everyone to see. Simply being a team member allows more anonymity for the quality of work and decisions made. If things don't work out in leadership, that person usually doesn't have the opportunity to move to another position within the company like a non-manager does.

2

Do It Anyway

Martina McBride's song *Do It Anyway* challenges us to do the right thing even when no one appreciates it. I urge you to take a break here and listen to the song (http://www.youtube.com/watch?v=SE3S7VcyOPU); it will inspire you and set the tone for the rest of this book. It is a call to service above self and embodies the message of *The Paradoxical Commandments*, which were written by Kent M. Keith at the tender age of 19. Read for yourself the wisdom beyond his years:

The Paradoxical Commandments

People are illogical, unreasonable, and self-centered.
Love them anyway.
If you do good, people will accuse you of selfish ulterior
  motives.
Do good anyway.
If you are successful, you will win false friends and true
  enemies.
Succeed anyway.
The good you do today will be forgotten tomorrow.
Do good anyway.
Honesty and frankness make you vulnerable.
Be honest and frank anyway.
The biggest men and women with the biggest ideas can
  be shot down by the smallest men and women with

the smallest minds.

Think big anyway.

People favor underdogs but follow only top dogs.

Fight for a few underdogs anyway.

What you spend years building may be destroyed overnight.

Build anyway.

People really need help but may attack you if you do help them.

Help people anyway.

Give the world the best you have and you'll get kicked in the teeth.

Give the world the best you have anyway.

3

Stewardship and Service above Self

Servant leadership is about caring for others more than for ourselves. It is about compassion for everyone who serves the group. It enriches everyone, not just those at the top. Servant leadership requires us to sit and weep with those who weep within our organizations. It requires getting down and dirty when hard work has to be done. There is nothing in my organization that anyone does that I should not be willing to do myself if it promotes the good of us all.

Hans Finzel, *The Top Ten Mistakes Leaders Make*

Stewardship of everything I have been entrusted with is a serious matter, one that I try not to take lightly. One day, I will have to answer for how I managed people within my sphere of influence, my money, and the organizational finances of companies I am involved in. I have a duty to look for ways to coach and speak into teachable moments with my family, team members, close friends, and peers. Real leaders give oversight to a group or organization's finances, people, and resources as if they were their own, even if they don't have legal or financial ownership.

When I mention service, you might think of a servant being forced to do some menial, manual labor. You might think of service as demeaning and weak. I submit to you that sincere service shows true strength of character. Being others-focused instead of self-focused changes your worldview. Living in a selfless manner and seeking to help others enriches our very existence on a daily basis. Get your hands dirty once in a while by serving in a capacity that is lower than your position or station in life. This keeps you tethered to the real world and grounded to reality, which should make it harder to be prideful and forget where you came from.

A leader knows the way, shows the way, and goes the way.

John Maxwell

There are very few who would dispute that Mother Theresa was a selfless leader. What was so remarkable about a woman who lived among poor people in the slums of Calcutta, India, and served them every day? How could that possibly be worth talking about enough that she became a household name across the globe? It is the result of her humbly "serving the one," and the rarity of that. Even if we have compassion for someone, it is much more common to give money to an organization to help them than to do the tangible work ourselves. We don't get physically involved in the situation at the source. We give some money and can think we are doing good works. Please don't misunderstand: I do think that giving money to charitable organizations that are making a difference is a necessary and good thing. But I often wonder, "Am I giving money as a means to avoid helping others directly and physically to meet their needs?" We need to both give money to help others and get involved in meeting those needs in a physical way. The latter is what made Mother Theresa so remarkable, since very few of us do this regularly. I challenge us to get out and "serve the one" more often.

It must often be so, Sam, when things are in danger: someone has to give them up, lose them, so that others may keep them.

J. R. R. Tolkien, *The Return of the King*

Serving the one requires us to be active when others are passive. We must resist the "bystander effect" and its accompanying "diffusion of responsibility" that is pervasive among public groups of people.

Wikipedia defines the bystander effect as

a social psychological phenomenon that refers to cases where individuals do not offer any means of help in an emergency situation to the victim when other people are present. The probability of help has often appeared to be inversely related to the number of bystanders; in other words, the greater the number of bystanders, the less likely it is that any one of them will help. The mere presence of other bystanders greatly decreases intervention. In general, this is believed to happen because as the number of bystanders increases, any given bystander is less likely to notice the situation, interpret the incident as a problem, and less likely to assume responsibility for taking action.

Wikipedia also defines the diffusion of responsibility as

a sociopsychological phenomenon whereby a person is less likely to take responsibility for an action or inaction when others are present. Considered a form of attribution, the individual assumes that either others are responsible for taking action or have already done so. The phenomenon tends to occur in groups of people above a certain critical size and when responsibility is not explicitly assigned. It rarely occurs when the person is alone, and diffusion increases with groups of three or more.

We are either afraid to take a risk and be made fun of, or we tell ourselves the lie that someone else will get involved and help. This video (http://youtu.be/KIvGI-wLcIuw) depicts, in painful detail, what happens when those present during a crime or crisis choose to allow evil to prevail, despite having sufficient numbers to stop the horrible crime happening before their eyes. Even when no one else will, choose to act, even if that means you will put your life in danger or risk overreacting and looking stupid. There is nothing nobler than sacrificing yourself for another, and so what if we get embarrassed by overreacting.

A quick decision is better than delay and indecision. Better to make a decision on info you have and adjust later if you need to.

Louisiana Governor Bobby Jindal

The best leaders communicate early and often during a crisis. Quick and decisive actions are warranted during emergencies whether they happen in politics or business. Contrary to popular belief, delay only makes things worse. Governor Bobby Jindal has a solid book called *Leadership and Crisis* that I highly recommend. It details his experience guiding Louisiana through the crises of the Deepwater Horizon oil disaster and Hurricane Gustav and is a breath of fresh air in the political arena.

Some leaders get that "deer in the headlights" look when confronted with crisis, while others tend to see things more clearly. I am blessed to be among the latter, and while that doesn't mean I make all the right decisions, I make them quickly and unequivocally. Then as the crisis unfolds, I make adjustments, sometimes reversing previous decisions. People might think that having to reverse yourself is bad management, but practically speaking, it is much better than delay, indecision, and lack of communication. Just ask any of the branches of the U.S. Armed Forces, who live and die by quick decisions. Delay and indecision can cost lives. Perhaps if our life depended on our decisions, we wouldn't delay so long in making decisions for our team members in business.

4

Skip Your Midlife Crisis

Our legacy in business and life is almost entirely defined by the type of people we hire and/or associate with.

Do you want to know the secret to avoiding the midlife crisis? Think about your legacy from the time you start your career and take a consistent role in creating intentional action along every step of the way to that end. As Stephen Covey puts it, "Begin with the end in mind." Many of us wait until we are in our 50s, 60s, or later to even start thinking about what our legacy will be, let alone to begin doing anything about it. Get involved in giving/serving in areas where you have talents; perhaps there are others you can mentor in a particular area within or outside your company. There may be boards you can serve on, soup kitchens you can give your time to, or many other service-oriented endeavors. Don't wait until you have enough time or money; the truth is there will always be a little more money to earn or a few more activities to pick up that limit service opportunities. Don't make excuses—start serving now. If you have kids, one benefit from engaging at a younger age is that your kids will catch you serving and mentoring others when you don't even realize it. This is something your children will not forget. Remember that they will imitate what they see you doing, not necessarily what you tell them to do. Have you heard the saying "Monkey see, monkey do"? We need to be aware of the influence we have, since leaders will always be held to a higher standard. People watch us as leaders, especially when we least expect it, and we usually get so caught up in the moment that we lose sight of the fact that others are acutely watching our every move. We must be consciously aware of our actions and choose to exemplify positive leadership traits. When we do make mistakes, we must recognize them and ask others' forgiveness for our shortcomings. Most people are quick to forgive if we are quick to say we are wrong and change our behavior.

One way to focus our lives on "beginning with the end in mind" is to write a personal and/or family mission statement. Stephen Covey, in his book *Seven Habits of Highly Successful People*, describes how significant it is to have a personal and family mission statement. I completely agree with his assessment. A mission statement serves as a compass to point us to "true north." Leading an organization can be like taking a hike through wooded hills. We're trying to go somewhere, but we can't get there in a straight line. As the path twists up and down the hills, it's easy to lose our bearings. In these situations, our stated mission is what keeps us moving toward our destination. Everything we do can and should be measured against the mission; does taking this step line up with it? My personal mission statement is "To Chart the Course, Pave the Pathway, and Light the Lane for Others to Eclipse My Own Leadership Success." I chose this mission statement because I see my role as one who will wield a machete in order to clear the obscure, overgrown brush in leadership and shine the light on the path to show others the way to achieve greater things than I have. Our family mission is the *Paradoxical Commandments* by Kent M. Keith (see chapter 2, "Do It Anyway").

We shouldn't allow our career, titles, or roles to define who we are as a person. Allowing ourselves to be defined by the roles we fill (father, physician, daughter, teacher, lawyer, cook, salesman, machinist, etc.) will only lead to disappointment when we screw up at or get fired at one or all of them. And we are all bound to make mistakes at some point due to our imperfect nature. This is a touchy one for me, since I have always wanted to be perfect at everything I do. I desire to know everything about leading and managing people and am not content to afford myself some slack for my shortcomings. I know I am not and can't be perfect, but I still have that inner drive to be perfect. Allowing our entire self-worth to be wrapped up in one or more of the roles we fill will virtually ensure a mid-life crisis.

5

Seek First to Understand, Then to Be Understood

If you're like most people, you probably seek first to be understood; you want to get your point across. And in doing so, you may ignore the other person completely, pretend that you're listening, selectively hear only certain parts of the conversation or attentively focus on only the words being said, but miss the meaning entirely.

Stephen Covey

Great leaders ask great, thoughtful questions. We all have a strong desire to be understood, but we have a responsibility to our team to listen first. We must resist the urge to force people to hear us by the power of our persona or position of authority. If our team makes a mistake, we should ask questions about what went wrong in the process. We might be surprised to learn the mistake was actually caused by us. And even if someone else did make a mistake, the truth of what happened will almost always be more complex than our simplistic assumptions that gave rise to our vitriolic anger and outburst. I first heard of this concept from Stephen Covey's book, *Seven Habits of Highly Successful People.* I must say, though, that I struggle with this in practice. We all have the tendency to listen just enough to jump in and offer our recommendation/ solution. We rarely listen to the other person fully before weighing in with our astute advice. Until we have listened and actually understand the situation, we have not earned the right to speak into the other's life. And even after listening attentively, we must be careful not to think too highly of our opinions.

And a simple way to understand others is to work hard at remembering their names. Sadly, remembering people's names is a lost art in American culture; we move too quickly through life and don't take the time to even learn the most basic details of others' lives. Or we make an excuse that we "aren't good with names." When I start working with a new group, my goal is to master at least 50 names in the first two weeks. It's obviously easier to learn all the names at a smaller company (which is where I have most of my experience), but working on a set amount of names per week allows me to scale up to whatever size the company may be. I can tell you from experience that remembering someone's name makes a dramatic impression; it shows that you care enough to take the time to focus on people. This is one of the simplest ways to quickly earn some initial respect and credibility. My mentor in this area is Dr. Raj Basu. He was one of the professors in my MBA program at Oklahoma State University, and he could master names even faster than I have ever achieved. By the end of the first meeting of our Organizational Theory class, he learned everyone's names (the class had over 40 students) and was able to repeat them back to the class without any prompting. Think about what an impact that had on me and my fellow classmates. He instantly earned a higher level of respect because he showed us he cared enough to learn our names. This is a simple, yet rare idea that always has an outsized impact.

Maturity doesn't come with age; it comes with acceptance of responsibility.

Edwin Louis Cole

Don't dismiss leadership simply on the basis of youth or inexperience. Often younger but talented people are denied opportunities to lead because they haven't "paid their dues." This is usually an excuse for those in power to hold on to power merely for control's sake, which is almost always rooted in insecurity of some kind. Fear of losing control is insecurity at its core. I want to learn until the day I die, and I want to gain knowledge from both young and old. It is important to give upcoming leaders chances to be out front, not trying to tightly and vainly cling to our own position of power. Assuming that those younger than us don't have wisdom is extremely arrogant. It is foolish to assume that acumen comes solely from someone with years of experience or grey hair. We must choose to discern whether others we come in contact with have something of value to offer us before we dismiss their leadership. This is a tricky one; you might be surprised at who is the superior leader if you only look at appearances.

When I meet someone that I think is in high school, I intentionally assume they are older and more mature than they appear. I usually ask them if they are a junior or senior in college. This is a habit that I have to work on—to correct my own first impressions of someone's age by assuming they are older or more mature than they appear to me. There are a number of reasons to do this. First, as I've gotten older, my first impressions of someone's age have skewed younger ("We didn't look that young when *we* were in high school, did we?"), so some correction is necessary. Second, if I overshoot the correction, the person will probably be gratified that I thought they were more mature than they actually are. By showing them respect, I will elicit trust and respect in turn and avoid the pitfall of underestimating their abilities and failing to tap into their potential. This can be a problem even when we know exactly how old someone is. We have to allow others room for growth. We shouldn't pigeonhole them at a certain age or maturity and lock them into those expectations for the rest of their life. This happens all too often and blinds us to their potential growth. Most of us have a tendency to look down on those younger than us, since we assume we have more experience, knowledge, or smarts than do they. If we don't keep an open mind, we will miss hiring or getting to know people who are wise beyond their years.

Leaders are more powerful role models when they learn than when they teach.

Rosabeth Moss Kantor

People who are avid learners seek out know-how wherever they can which makes them smarter and contributes to better results.

David Novak

Another way to understand others and the world around us is to continually read and learn. Leaders should be readers.[2] It is up to us to learn and explore the world more deeply and apply that knowledge for the benefit of our family, friends, and work environment. I am glad you are reading this book, but I hope you read other books on a variety of subjects in order to give you a well-rounded view of the world. I happen to be highly intrigued by the following subjects: economics, leadership/management, classical and contemporary music, business history, new technology/science, Christian theology/apologetics (especially the debate between Calvinism and Arminianism), marketing, board/corporate governance, marriage enrichment, and the classical method of education (as opposed to a progressive one).

What are you interested in?

6

Leadership Pacing

Stay one step ahead of your people, and you are called a leader. Stay ten steps ahead of your people and you are called a martyr!

Allowing ourselves to run too far ahead of our team only leaves them in the dust; they cannot follow what they cannot keep up with. Most visionary, creative leaders have minds that process things quickly and intuitively. If we aren't careful to slow down a bit and explain the intuitive leaps, our unprepared organizations will go off half-cocked. Without the entire organization rallied to the task, we will muddle through and execute poorly rather than with excellence. This doesn't mean we have to move at a snail's pace either; our team members may have to speed up a bit. Just be careful not to be Speedy Gonzales.[3]

If everything's a rush, then nothing is. If we ask too often for things to be done last minute, we risk giving our team the perception that everything is last minute. At that point, the team will have little motivation to respond to really time-sensitive tasks. Moreover, we risk the team losing confidence in our ability to lead. Have a little respect for your team and ask for things to be rushed infrequently, only when they genuinely need to be expedited. Then you must match your own behavior to your expectations by responding to your team in as rapid a fashion as you expected of them. Don't delay your approval or revisions; answer your team as quickly as you expected them to get you the initial information. It will build trust by demonstrating that you will hold yourself to the same standard and will respect their time.

Don't get caught up in the tyranny of the supposed urgent. Reevaluate your priorities regularly; if you don't, you will get swept away in the deluge of "urgent" work that floods your desk. Some purportedly pressing stuff actually isn't, and it is up to us as leaders to discern the difference between the two. Craig Groeschel, Pastor of LifeChurch.tv, suggests limiting the number of tasks you are engaged in and using the extra hours for more productive tasks. I know that at times I get my head down and keep the same routine, when I should stop to reevaluate my schedule and refocus on the areas of greatest importance or influence. We owe it to ourselves and others to sit down at least once a quarter to reevaluate what is truly exigent in our lives and business and prune out the superfluous involvements. Learning how to stop doing things is more important than learning how to start; most of us don't seem to have a problem with the latter.

Don't be a bottleneck. If a matter is not a decision for the President or you, delegate it. Force responsibility down and out. Find problem areas, add structure and delegate. The pressure is to do the reverse. Resist it.

Donald Rumsfeld

Great leaders take the time to respond to their team with answers that are both quick and well thought out. Otherwise, the team grows weary of waiting on an answer. Our family, co-workers, and team members deserve better, so let's not slow them down from doing the job we have assigned them to do. How many times do we ask someone to do a job, then we (usually unintentionally) delay making the decisions that would allow them to complete the job? We asked them to do it, we're paying them to do it, but we're not letting them do it! Isn't that ironic?[4] Too often, we are the bottleneck of our organization. It is more often than not the leader's fault, not the team member's. We need to prioritize our own work schedule to keep others efficient and effective with their time. If we don't have the time to give people a response, we need to delegate more of our decisions to others.

It drives me crazy when another driver chooses to drive slowly in the left lane, especially when there is another slower driver in the right lane going the exact same speed. Now, I don't mind if people want to drive slowly, but please don't hold the rest of us back just because you can or are not paying attention. This is applicable both in driving cars and in business. Many of us do this without even thinking or paying attention; we become that "driver in the left lane with the left blinker that has been on for the last 20 minutes." This is terribly inconsiderate, and most leaders don't even realize it until team members start quitting in significant numbers. If we as leaders can't keep pace with others, then we owe it to the group to either speed up by increasing our efficiency or decreasing our procrastination. If we can do neither, then we must pull over, metaphorically speaking, by either delegating better or letting others lead. It is the only sane thing to do for the group. Please lead, follow, or get out of the way.

7

Delegation and Short-Term Pain, Long-Term Gain

Don't tell people how to do things; tell them what to do and let them surprise you with their results.

General George Patton

We need to *macro*manage, not *micro*manage by focusing on managing the macro details and trusting others to focus on the minutiae. Without focus on the bigger picture, our organizations reach a certain plateau of success and begin to stagnate. And as top leaders micromanage, they get lost in the details that don't matter as much (e.g., dress code, how often people use the internet/e-mail, minimal overtime pay, small individual expenses, etc.) and fail to monitor larger, critical trends (e.g., cash flow, profitability, expense, COGS, revenue, and industry trends) and make proactive changes to anticipate those coming trend changes. In order for our companies to grow, we must continually delegate and entrust more and more micro-level decisions to middle managers, so we can focus on managing the larger financial numbers and vision/ strategy of the organization.

> I'd rather get ten men to do the job than to do the job of ten men.

D. L. Moody

Proper delegation of duties and responsibilities will allow people to learn by failure. If you don't delegate, you are refusing to allow them to learn and grow. Many of us don't understand the value of delegation; we believe that we can do it more accurately and speedily than taking the tedious time to train someone else. This is true in the short term, but not in the long run. If the person is skilled and capable of learning the task you need done, delegation is the more efficient route. Without delegation, our organizations will remain stagnant and resistant to growth. This is purely a lesson in delaying gratification: By taking the extra time to train someone, you will reap higher productivity in your own work or life, focusing on tasks that fit your passions and skills.

Sometimes we need to make a decision ourselves, but more often it is proper to encourage other team members to make the decision (assuming they have been trained properly). I have a saying that I picked up somewhere (I can't remember to whom to attribute it). When a decision has to be made about a certain situation, I will say to the team members who are closest to the situation, "You have a 50/50 chance of being right; I have only a 10 percent chance at best." Those numbers might seem startling, but I believe them to be true. And the farther up the management/leadership chain we are (and further away from the actual job/task being done), the lower our odds of coming to the right conclusion. We should encourage those closest to the situation to make most of the decisions.

Lack of delegation is an example of trading short-term gain for long-term pain. Most people choose the short term over the long term every day by default, since they don't even consider the possibilities for sacrificing now to gain later on. My guess is that when you fully comprehend the ramifications of this concept, it will intuitively make sense. We need leaders who choose to trade short-term pain for long-term gain. This is a selfless act involving delaying gratification. Saving money rather than spending it, paying down debt rather than increasing it, and driving a "beater" car rather than a new one are all examples of trading short-term pain for long-term gain. In the long run, you will be out of debt and can afford to pay cash for a new vehicle if you choose. Paying for private education for your children takes sacrifice in the short term, so that in the long term, your kids will be better educated and prepared for their career, relationships, finances, etc. There are many more applications in personal and business life as well as politics. So many organizations are filled with people who focus only on doing the least they can do to keep their job, rather than setting up their company for future success long after they retire. When making decisions, stop and ask yourself whether you are trading short-term gain for long-term pain. Also think of how this affects others, not just yourself. And when you choose to delegate, don't reverse course. It does more damage than not delegating in the first place.

8

Empowerment

He that thinketh he leadeth and hath no one following him only taketh a walk.

John Maxwell

Abdication isn't empowerment. Have you ever met a leader that talked a lot about empowering others? Most who talk about it merely give it lip service or use a simplistic definition of the word. Let's look at what the dictionary says. TheFreeDictionary.com defines *empowerment* as follows:

1. To invest with power, especially legal power or official authority.
2. To equip or supply with an ability.

To invest in someone or equip them with an ability implies *action* on the part of the leader. What a novel concept! Many leaders think that empowering others means walking away from the situation and letting their followers sink or swim. We often figuratively or literally say, "Good luck!" thinking our leadership duty is done, but it's not. We are either ignorant of the need for us to actively participate in empowerment, or we choose to be lazy, since true empowerment takes a lot of work. In order to empower others, we must define the power and

authority they have in decision making. I liken this to
setting guardrails on a task or project being delegated; it
is our job as a leader to define what we want them to
do—and more importantly, what we don't want them to
do. Then we must define what types of choices they can
make without our involvement and what decisions they
must bring to us for input. Then they have been genuinely empowered, since we have properly equipped and
invested in them first.

People can't be empowered without the proper
resources to do their job. Equip your soldiers with the
tools they need to do the job you've asked of them. We
have all been guilty of this one; we have sent our team
members off to complete a task when we haven't given
them the tools to effectively and efficiently do it.
Resources can take many forms: computers, software,
money, cross-departmental support, other equipment, or
even pay. Whether they realize the cause or not, a team
sent out unequipped will slowly lose respect for leadership
because we won't give them the basic tools they need to
do the job. It's ironic, isn't it? I realize that no organization has unlimited funding; we can't give our team members the moon. But we should find ways to equip them as
much as possible. Don't use excuses; focus on the solution.
Sometimes that might mean spending your own money
to ensure your team's success. It might mean starving a
pet project that the leader is energized by, but isn't profitable, in order to give the team what it needs to work
more effectively. That's not what we want to hear, but it
might just be the cold, hard fact. With the proper tools,
our team members become less stressed and more at ease
in their work.

> Authority without responsibility is tyranny, and responsibility without authority is impotence.

Peter Drucker

Don't give someone responsibility without the requisite authority. When we hire managers to oversee others, we often want to give them the authority. But we either can't/won't let go of control, or we are afraid others will make wrong decisions without our input. If we aren't willing to give someone authority, then we shouldn't bestow responsibility. We should just do it all ourselves, never delegate, and frustrate our team until all of the top performers leave and all the "yes-men" create so much dysfunction in the team that we eventually capitulate to slowdown, shutdown, or bankruptcy. Before entrusting responsibility to another, ask yourself whether you're prepared to give them the authority to act, or whether you will undercut their power at every turn. In either case, we need to learn to allow others the authority to discharge the responsibility they have been given as a leader.

> Independent thinking alone is not suited to interdependent reality. Independent people who do not have the maturity to think and act interdependently may be good individual producers, but they won't be good leaders or team players. They're not coming from the paradigm of interdependence necessary to succeed in marriage, family, or organizational reality.

Stephen Covey

We can only empower a team of people who view interdependence as the aim, not independence or co-dependence.

Especially in America, where the very establishment of our country was based on independence, we are too focused on making it alone in this world. We rarely see the need or use for reliance on others. And I would argue that we shouldn't go to the other extreme of co-dependence. Independence is the sole reliance on oneself. Dependence is total reliance on someone else, and co-dependence is the inability of two or more people to function without the other. Interdependence is a healthy relationship of mutual dependency for which we need to shoot. For example, as children we start out dependent on our parents; then we move to the next stage of either independence or co-dependence, usually in our late teens or early twenties. And lastly we either choose to stay independent/co-dependent in our adult lives or move to the final phase of maturity, interdependence with our family and as well as our peers, co-workers, and friends.

9

Laziness vs. Workaholism

Pick up the phone or walk across the office. E-mail can
be a wonderful business tool, but I think that many times
it gets in the way of good communication. I don't think
there are hard and fast rules when it comes to the type of
communication we should use. But if an e-mail conversation has bounced back and forth more than a couple of
times, it is time to pick up the phone or walk over to that
person's office and have an actual conversation. Texting,
e-mail, and social media communication make us feel like
we're in a super-connected world. But sometimes we need
to break free from the latest technology, recognizing that
some communication is better in person or on the phone.
The convenience of communicating over various techno-
logical shortcuts comes at the expense of body language,
tone of voice, eye movement, and facial expressions. And
since research tells us that at least 60% of communication
is nonverbal,[5] we should be able to see the limitation of
sole or even heavy reliance on digitized communication.

Laziness/selfishness is a choice. We are all naturally
selfish, even those who choose to live a selfless life. We
are all naturally lazy, even those who choose to live a reg-
imented, highly productive life. Those who are outwardly
unselfish and/or industrious choose to practice unselfish
and hard-working behavior; both are habits that must be
worked on daily. It takes time to develop these habits to
the point where, like a child who has practiced riding a

bike many times, you can enact the behavior almost naturally. But over time you still must hone your skills lest they get rusty. I compare this to my violin and viola performing. While I have played for over 30 years, if I don't practice regularly, my performance starts to lose its polish. The difference between those who are selfish and those who are selfless, or between those who are lazy and those who are productive, is not in their natural inclinations; the difference is the discipline in their daily actions.

Relationship is spelled T-I-M-E.

Workaholism is worse than alcoholism. What do you choose more often, time or money? Most people would say they value time over money, but our actions often say differently. We routinely work extra hours to make more money or advance our careers rather than leave work to spend time with our families and friends. While we do need money to live and provide for our families, we only have one life to live. I have never heard anyone later in life look back and say, "Man, I wish I had had more money." They always wish they had spent more time with their kids, wife, parents, and friends. Time with others should always come first if we must choose between the two. If we can have both, then all the better. And in order to have more time, sometimes money can even be used to buy us more time. A great example of this is when we hire team members to work for us and take a load of work off our plate, so we can either focus on other more valuable work or simply have more time to spend with those closest to us.

Most business-minded people, especially entrepreneurs, believe the lie that we must work 70–90 hours a week to succeed, but it is simply not true. And much has been said and written about work-life balance, some even suggesting at the other end of the spectrum that only 4 hours a week is necessary. But there is no consensus about what a proper work-life balance looks like precisely. Certainly, there are those who work too many hours that are prosperous financially, but most of them have terrible family and personal lives (divorces, estranged children, etc.). Defining the right balance is a subjective decision, but there are some tools to help you gauge how you're doing. One question you can ask of those family and friends closest to you is, "Do I spend enough time with you doing the things you find fascinating?" Make sure that work doesn't take precedence over your spouse, kids, or other important people in your life. There will be occasions where your company legitimately needs you to work an evening or weekend. Just don't allow it to be out of balance either way. Time spent with your family and friends is eternal and cannot be retrieved once lost. We need to choose to honor our family and our health by limiting our hours to no more than 40–50 hours per week on average. Sometimes work will require more than that, but let's not allow the long hours to go on for more than a week or two. We should only allow short bursts of this extra effort before patterning back into a more sustainable pace. By limiting our hours of work, we can focus on rest and play; it also forces us to be more efficient with our time and prioritize things more effectively. Working fewer hours more efficiently paradoxically shakes us out of laziness. Leaving the office at a set time each night might be a hard habit to start, but trust me, the work will be there tomorrow, and most of the work CAN wait until tomorrow. One of my life goals is to have no regrets in this area.

Giving team members permission to unplug is vital to

work-life balance. The people that work for us should
know that we don't want them at our beck and call even
during their off hours. Let your team have their evenings
and weekends to themselves and only interrupt them if
it is truly urgent. They should hear from you that even
if you send them an e-mail during their off hours, they
are not expected to complete the tasks right away unless
you explicitly say so. Routinely ask them how they are
doing with work-life balance to help them establish good
patterns and hold them accountable. We need to avoid
giving them the impression that we expect them to be
available to work 24/7/365. If you *have* been expecting
them to work all the time, please make it clear that things
have changed. Otherwise you will burn them out, and a
burned-out worker is an inefficient worker, one who will
probably leave your employ sooner than you think.

10

Sacrifice, Silence, and Solitude

There is no greater love than to lay down one's life for
one's friends.

John 15:13, NLT

It is regrettable that sacrifice is so conspicuously absent
in our culture. There are a few exceptions, most notably
the military. Young men and women routinely place their
lives on the line in deployment to various battlefields
around the world. This is the antithesis of selfishness. I
wish we had more people following the mantra of self-
sacrifice. But it does no good to despair or to use this as
an excuse not to lead. Sacrifice is noble and inspirational
to others around you, so please find ways to elevate the
needs of others and lessen the importance of your own.
Firefighters are a perfect model for sacrifice; they run into
a burning building risking their life to save others, not
knowing if they will come out alive. Leaders take the hit
for their followers. If your team members are bearing the
brunt of whatever hardships come to your organization,
you're shirking your responsibility.

I have grown to appreciate the disciplines of silence
and solitude. I first became aware of the power of silence
in my music studies. I have studied classical music most
of my life; I compose music and play violin and viola.

When I was learning to compose, I discovered that inexperienced composers vainly rush to fill every moment of the piece with notes. They overload the page to show off their composing prowess and neglect the power of rests (the silence between two notes). The more experienced composer uses fewer notes and more strategically placed silences. This applies to our lives as well; we must find times of silence and solitude to reflect and break through the noise of life.

Solitude doesn't always bring peace in the way we would expect. A couple of years ago, I camped by myself at a secluded campground a hundred miles out of town. Simply getting away from everything (family, friends, entertainment, and other city comforts) overnight was one of the most refreshing, yet unsettling times I can recall. There was no one to talk to, no phone or computer to connect with others, and lots of silence. This wasn't easy for me; I am a highly self-motivated and driven individual with high goals, aspirations, and many commitments. That silence drove me nuts, since I am always thinking and multitasking at a hundred miles per hour. But we don't often discipline our mind to slow down in order to more deliberately focus on what is most important. There is something in the practice of silence and solitude that recharges us and helps us get clarity and perspective. Sometimes we can't see the forest for the trees, and we just need silence and solitude to help elucidate our situation.

11

Generosity, Not Greed

The greedy leader will sacrifice the good of the organization for the sake of personal advancement. Greedy leaders have a difficult time moving others into the spotlight, will change the rules in the middle of the game, and are reluctant to share the credit and rewards of success.

Andy Stanley

I owe a "hat tip" to *The Andy Stanley Leadership Podcast*[6] for this one. Being generous is harder than it seems; it is much easier to act out of greed. Greed pervades our consumer culture, and it is the hardest to detect in ourselves. We want a larger house, better car, more money, or a more powerful position at work. But a more insidious and subtle form of greed relates to the way we treat people. And the only antidote to greed, in any form, is intentional generosity in those specific areas where we struggle. Perhaps you tend to think the worst of people instead of giving them the benefit of the doubt. Or maybe you pinch pennies when it comes to your spouse's spending habits but are unwilling to cut your own favorite budget items. Or it could take the form of withholding your time from your children, even unintentionally. Perhaps you are generous to everyone except your family or except in certain other circumstances? Do you encourage others enough? Do you look for ways to reward team member performance, or do you struggle with giving pay raises? Do you think team members are lucky to have a job at your company, or do you look for ways to help them develop even if they might eventually get a better job with another firm? Do you pay your vendors late in order to smooth out cash flow? These are all signs of greed and lack of respect for others. If you struggle in any of these or similar areas, you will have to deliberately develop habits that undermine greed. Keep in mind that your own greed is the hardest to spot, so if you don't think you have a greed problem, you probably haven't looked close enough.

Generally speaking, we should do good works in secret so that our rewards are eternal (see Matthew 6:1-4), but we must not hide all of these works from those closest to us. If we hide all our good deeds, then our spouse, children, and close friends will never learn from our example. And let's face it, we learn more from the example of those closest to us than from anything else. So strategically allow a few to participate in the good things you do for others, so they will in turn follow your exemplary behavior. Just remember to keep your pride in check by not showing off too many of your good works, or your reward will be the temporal affirmation of others, not eternal.

Neither ignore nor abuse the norm of reciprocity. The norm of reciprocity is the social expectation that others will return benefits for benefits without the giver expecting anything directly in return. Paying for lunch or coffee for someone is a simple and yet powerful way to build trust with another person. You'd be surprised at how few people actually do something like this for others without expectation of return. If you focus only on what you will get from giving, you are abusing the norm and will gain very little in the long run for your trouble. But make no mistake, most people will respond to genuine generosity in kind as there is a subconscious social pressure to return the favor at some point in the future. While we shouldn't expect something in return, if we are generous, there will be a return the vast majority of the time. But it might be unseen. Be careful; you might be surprised at how generous others can be. And don't worry that people will think you're being generous just to get something in return. If you are sincere, your authenticity will be borne out over time.

It's harder to receive than give.

Dan Allender

Did you catch that? Some of us do struggle with giving, but at times, our pride gets in the way of receiving. Do you have a hard time allowing someone else to pay for lunch or a movie? Or is it hard to accept an unexpected gift? Would it be unthinkable to rely on someone to give you cash if you had financial troubles? If so, then consider the likelihood that pride is getting in the way of allowing others to be generous. I have created a habit in my life that if someone offers to pay for something or give me a gift, I just say, "Thank you."

Most of us, myself included, don't want anyone to know when we struggle financially. When I was out of a job a few years ago, my wife and I decided to open ourselves up to criticism by sending a weekly e-mail to our close friends, soliciting their prayers for specific financial needs we had. I was surprised at all the support (financial, emotional, and spiritual) that our friends provided. One particular friend helped us pay our mortgage and then gave me a job mowing lawns for his rental properties. He was initially nervous about asking me to do the lawn moving, thinking it might be beneath me, but I was humbled that he would reach out to us in such a generous fashion and was grateful for the part-time job to bring in any income. One night during that time of unemployment, our kids asked if we could have pizza, and I had to tell them that we simply didn't have the money to buy pizza. No one outside our family knew about the discussion, but someone from our church brought us pizza that very night. I believe God provides for us in the smallest ways to let us know He cares about seemingly small things. Whether the provision is great or small, the proper response to the grace of God is to accept it with gratitude. If we allow ourselves to receive from others, then it becomes easier to give.

The superior man blames himself. The inferior man blames others.

Don Shula

Another way to show generosity is to seek the blame and give away the fame. A culture of blame and excuse-making is dangerous because it stops people from learning from their mistakes and leads to more errors. Our first inclination is to blame someone or something else for failure. Now, someone else may or may not deserve blame. It may well be that your predecessor left you in circumstances that directly contributed to the current crisis. But shifting blame skips over the pertinent question we must ask ourselves: "What could I have done better?" We shouldn't allow ourselves to use excuses ("circumstances beyond my control . . ."), even if they are valid ones. Focus on what we can influence or change. We all love to shift blame to someone else or circumstances beyond our control, especially when we are thrust into a crisis. Resist the urge and seek the blame.

Now, the second part of this is to give away the fame, and this is equally hard. The team should get the credit from their leaders for success, and the leaders get to shoulder the weight of blame for failure. Great head coaches and quarterbacks in the NFL emulate this during the postgame press conference after a loss. They accept responsibility for not better preparing/leading the team. And when they win, they deflect credit from themselves and project it onto teammates, assistant coaches, etc. They have trained themselves to lead selflessly, even if others were at fault for the failure. Ascribe acclaim to other team members or the entire team whenever there is credit to be taken. You will build a strong sense of loyalty among your team if you seek the blame and give away the fame.

12

Wrap-up

Denying our selfish nature and intentionally placing ourselves in the position of servitude is both counter to human nature and to our current culture. Beginning in the '60s and '70s and growing stronger through the present day, we have a culture that more and more says, "Do what feels good for you. Only your happiness matters. Love yourself. Follow your heart. If it feels right to you, it's right." What it never explicitly states but certainly implies is that we should ignore others' needs. Sacrifice, generosity, service, and delayed gratification are by and large not valued today, and we need to change that. True happiness doesn't result from loving ourselves and fulfilling every one of our own desires, it comes from serving others, and sadly many of us live our whole lives on a quest for self-fulfillment that leads to disappointment, disillusionment, and discontentment.

PART 2

Do What's Best for Your Organization

Leadership is as much about putting others first as it is about making the tough decisions. Unlike how we romanticize being in management, choosing to lead and do what's best for your organization is not a walk in the park. It involves stress, interruption, conflict, and burdensome responsibility. How we develop and nurture the culture within our organizations and family is vital to others' success as well as ours. Hiring, coaching, and retaining the right people in our organizations is the single largest influence we have over our organizations' culture.

13

Embrace Negotiation, Overcommunication, and Interruptions

Negotiate fairly, face-to-face, and without attorneys or other intermediaries. I don't want to suggest that you should ignore sound legal or financial advice, but once you have received the professionals' advice, it is much simpler for the decision makers to meet one-on-one to hammer out the details of an agreement. Most attorneys and CPAs are paid to cover every possible angle and remove all risk from the transaction. Removing *most* of the risk is smart business. But all deals require some calculated risk, or there would be no reward. Involving attorneys and CPAs in the actual negotiations throws up barriers to mutually beneficial agreements. So step up to the leadership plate, become informed by your advisors, but then negotiate as directly as possible with the other decision maker. Most of the time the result is a more candid conversation around the most important issues, and an agreement can be reached more quickly.

Putting things in writing is liberating not limiting. We are afraid of putting things on paper in a formal agreement. The only explanation for this I can fathom is that we are afraid either of commitment or the consequences of violating the letter of the law. In my experience, it is quite liberating to know with contractual certainty what each party will do in a variety of situations. I understand that an agreement cannot possibly cover all the conceivable contingencies, but that is where the spirit of the law comes into play. Both parties enter the agreement in good faith and shouldn't intend to take advantage of the other. It is true that things get much stickier when one or both parties choose to violate the letter and/or spirit of the agreement, but at least we know what was agreed to. And if both parties follow the agreement, strong trust and relationship will result in a better future business relationship and/or partnership, which benefits shareholders, team members, and customers alike. If we don't formalize an agreement, there is undoubtedly more uncertainty than if we have one.

Preemptively negotiate to do what is fair. When your partner in some venture is getting the short end of the stick, it is tempting to ride that advantage as far as you can. It seems counterintuitive to renegotiate, but by doing so, you may gain more than you give. A company I previously managed was halfway into a four-month contract with the company developing our website, when our contact there let me know that the work was taking way more hours than anyone had anticipated. We could have gotten all we could out of them while they were locked into that contract. But rather than wait another two months to renegotiate terms (which we had every right to do contractually), we told them we would pay a significant additional sum on the current contract, and that it would be paid within the next week. Within minutes of us sending that e-mail, the owner called me to say that in over twenty years of business, he never had a customer do anything like this. He profusely thanked us for our generosity. Now, stop and think about this for a minute. The company didn't have to pay them any extra money, but I knew the right thing to do was to pay them before our contract came up for renewal. And while I knew it would gain us tremendous goodwill, that wasn't my primary motivation: The most important consideration was that it was what a servant leader would do. As a secondary benefit, we gained trust with that company. If I ever needed to ask them for a favor, they would probably bend over backward for us. Giving up the advantage is more powerful than we realize because it is so rare. I challenge you to try this. In the short term, it might be slightly painful, but in the long run, I can assure you it will pay off.

Don't overcharge or undercharge. I learned this from a neighbor when I lived in Tulsa, Oklahoma, several years ago. I have used it many times since. Plainly put, when you're negotiating a price with a vendor, instruct them to neither overcharge nor undercharge you and see what happens. I know it is a bit scary to expose yourself like that. But it works like magic; if you find out later that they took advantage of your trust and overcharged you, never refer them any business or do business with them yourself again. If they respect the vulnerability with which you approached them and treat you fairly, they will probably be grateful for the generosity, trust, and fairness you offered them in the relationship, making them more loyal and likely to go the extra mile for you.

In the vacuum created by a lack of communication, people tend to dream up and believe in the wildest explanations of fact.

We almost always overestimate the amount and sufficiency of our own communication. We fall short in this area due to our belief that people actually listen to us. In marketing, it takes a minimum of seven messages for the consumer to pay attention to a product or service. And that is just to get their attention. It can then take more time and information messages to convince them to purchase a product or service. We should have this same perspective when it comes to communicating with our team members in business. Not that we focus on their failure to listen, but rather we understand the responsibility we as leaders have to communicate important information multiple times. It is just part of the territory of being in leadership. This isn't to be used by our team members as an excuse not to be attentive and develop listening skills. Leaders and team members should each focus on how we can get better at communicating frequently and listening more intently.

And in the interest of overcommunicating, we must choose a path of up-front, full disclosure. People rarely have a problem with something, even a conflict of interest, as long as it is stated up front with full disclosure. But all kinds of problems result when we fail to communicate things up front, especially when there is even the appearance of a conflict of interest that others hear about after the fact. We must choose to remain vigilant in this area, so we earn a deeper level of trust with others and they know we will always do our best to avoid the appearance of abusing our authority/loyalty or conflict of interest. Common types of conflict of interest are self-dealing, outside employment, family interests, gifts from friends, and misuse of confidential information, all of which should be avoided.

As annoying as interruptions usually are at work and at home, we fail to realize that they are an inescapable and necessary facet of leadership. If you're a leader, interruptions aren't what keep you from your work; the interruptions *are* your work. To illustrate, think of a military leader in the heat of battle who is focused on the plan of war. When a soldier comes to the commander and says, "Sir, we are running out of ammunition," a good leader doesn't say, "I'm too busy right now; come back later." That would be absurd. Yet we as leaders tell our team members and family members either explicitly or implicitly (e.g., through body language) not to bother us with the seemingly trivial details of everyday work/life. We may even say verbally that we want people to interrupt us with smaller details but demonstrate the opposite by not being available when that time comes. We must realize that the interruption is actually an incredibly valuable exchange between leader and team member, an opportunity to get info from the front lines and give direction and counsel. It's a chance to make the entire team more successful. Most leaders are chosen because they are good at the technical work of the business but rarely because they are good at delegating and making decisions to enable the team to succeed.

The higher you go in leadership, the more problems you have to bear; it just comes with the territory. I love the scene in the movie *Saving Private Ryan* when Tom Hanks' character's unit asks him why they never hear him complaining about the lousy mission they are on to save Private Ryan. He responds, "I'm a captain, I don't gripe to my men. Gripes go up. Not down." You can be sure that the captain was carrying a huge burden of leadership on this mission.

Hans Finzel, *The Top Ten Mistakes Leaders Make*

Either do something about it or stop complaining. This is fairly self-explanatory concept but one that is hard for me to follow; if you have the authority, power, money, or influence, to change something, just change it! Don't complain about it. If you don't have the authority, power, money, or influence to change something, either ask for help from someone up the chain of command or give up grumbling. Venting your frustration to those closest to you is okay, but do it sparingly and move on. The world has enough incessant whiners.

> You do not have, because you do not ask.
>
> James 4:2, ESV

> Keep on asking, and you will receive what you ask for. Keep on seeking, and you will find. Keep on knocking, and the door will be opened to you.
>
> Matthew 7:7, NLT

Be pleasantly persistent. Don't be afraid to ask for something you assume your boss, friend, or co-worker wouldn't give you. Approach them with humility, not in a demanding way, and ask for their help. If at first you receive a "maybe," then be pleasantly persistent in your follow-up (unless they ask you to stop). Allow some time to elapse before following up so as not to be annoying. Keep in mind that few people actually follow up the second or third time, so you will already have an advantage. If they give you a definite no, then by all means stop bugging them unless you have new information that might change their decision. You just never know when your pleasant perseverance will pay off in a big way.

We should persevere but also know when to quit. Leaders should have persistence in their DNA, but they should also know when to throw in the towel. If a project, business relationship, or job becomes unprofitable (quantitatively or qualitatively), then stop investing in it. Most of us have a tendency to hang on too long, since we have so much time and money already invested. We must choose to look at those as sunk costs (past decisions) that don't have any bearing on today's decision on whether to continue. The only exception to this is if you have already committed yourself or your organization to something (either by formal agreement or simply by your word); in that case, you should keep your word, even if it costs you.

14

Team Culture: Hiring and Coaching People Who Fit

Culture eats strategy for breakfast.

Peter Drucker

What works for one company does not necessarily work for another, even in a similar industry. This is shown in the high failure rate of mergers. According to Heidrick & Struggles, a leadership advisory and consultancy group, 74% of mergers fail. The two reasons they fail are incompatible corporate cultures and poor leadership of the merged companies. Of course, just having a strong culture isn't a guarantee of success either; just ask Enron, World-Com, or Lehman Brothers. They all had extremely strong cultures built on greed, pride, and fraud. Nurturing the right kind of culture for your company is part art, part science, but the most important tactic is hiring the right kind of people for your type of culture. Then guard the doors to your organization ruthlessly, repelling anyone who doesn't fit. Now, this is easier said than done, and each organization must find ways that make sense for their company. Personally, I have found using motivation assessments helpful, most recently using the Flag Page® assessment. This assessment was created by a company I used to work for, primarily for marriage communication (www.flagpage.com). I feel that using this tool has brought me from being a "so-so" hiring manager to one that selected the right cultural fit a vast majority of the time.

> Hire smaller and we become company of dwarfs. By hiring people who are bigger, we become a company of giants.
>
> @OgilvyWW

Hire those smarter and more skilled than you are, and don't be intimidated by them. This is a tough one to learn, since we all have egos and desire to be the most skilled and smartest person in the room. In order for our organizations to grow, we must learn to humble ourselves by hiring better experts and more accomplished workers than we are. If we do follow this path, our organizations won't be limited by our own weaknesses and faults. This is exactly why most small businesses reach a ceiling and can't seem to break through it. They choose their own way of mediocrity because they can't humble themselves and recognize their organization's need for better leaders. If you find yourself in this spot, strongly consider whether you have passed up smarter and more talented people than you in favor of smaller and less gifted folks. If you have, it's not too late to stop this practice and start placing value on those who are more capable than you are. The truth is that there is always someone more gifted and adept than we are; we can choose to ignore or deny it, but it doesn't change the truth.

The world has enough mini-me's. How many of us have known a leader who surrounded himself with yes-men or mini-me's (followers who are exactly like him on a smaller scale)?[7] Unfortunately, we have all seen too much of this kind of leadership. Sadly, the weaknesses of that leader are amplified throughout the organization. If only people were hired that cover the leader's blind spots, the whole organization would be strengthened. When I hire, I am looking for someone with the right skills and the right cultural fit for the organization, but I intentionally guard against hiring mini-me's by interviewing with another trusted team member who is wired and motivated very differently from me. This doesn't mean we can't hire people that have similar values; it does mean we must guard against hiring an entire army of people whose skills, personalities, and strengths/weaknesses are too similar to the leader.

The difference between leadership and friendship means that sometimes you have to fire your best friend.

@JenAlsever

Nepotism isn't all bad—just mostly bad. In the majority of cases, it is terribly destructive to organizations and the individual family member's long-term employability, but there are some exceptions. If expectations are set up right from the beginning, and there is a healthy dose of respect and genuine accountability, there can be incredible strength from employing a family member, since there is a higher level of trust based on years of witnessing their character. If you want to hire a family member, ask yourself the following questions:

1. If I need to fire them in the future, for whatever

reason, will I not hesitate to do so?

2. Have they worked faithfully for someone else or another nonfamily company?
3. Do they have enough of the skills that are required for the position?
4. Do they fit the company culture we are trying to foster?

If you can honestly answer all of these with a resounding yes, then you are ready to take the first step to hiring them. The second step, and just as important as the first, is setting up guidelines/expectations on how you will work together. The business is not the same setting as the home, and the professional environment should change how you interact. For example, I used to work for my father, a dermatologist who owns a small pharmaceutical company. While on the job, I chose to call him Dr. Smith; he never asked me to, but it was a sign of respect to him and an implicit indication to all the other team members that I wasn't above the law. I put myself under the same rules as everyone else. In that instance, it was the team member who took the initiative, but it is important for the leader to clearly define the rules of engagement, so there are no misunderstandings on how things will work. Giving favoritism to anyone, especially family, is terribly destructive to team morale.

Good people do not need laws to tell them to act responsibly, while bad people will find a way around the laws.

Plato

Policies only work if we hire good people to follow them.

If we think we need to add more policies to fix a people problem, we are fooling ourselves. I will take good people over good policies any day of the week. Now, we might need to change policies, but this alone won't fix most issues. We must hire the right kind of people who will do the right thing for the business regardless of policies in place, their pay, or how they feel today. Sadly, these types of people are scarcer and harder to locate. But if you attract these sorts of people to your organization, you will build a strong, positive, nearly impenetrable culture that will reject the wrong type of people (i.e., the lying, gossiping, selfish variety). If you hire a team of good people, they will not want to leave, and the policies will mostly take care of themselves. Hire the wrong people, and it won't matter what policies you enact: The guidelines will never have the intended positive result.

Recruit, don't just post a job. Many people think they are "recruiting" for their organization by merely posting open positions on a job website like monster.com or careerbuilder.com. But this is only one of many tools in the human resources toolbox. And then those same people complain profusely to their colleagues that "good people are so hard to find these days." Merely posting a job is highly unlikely to uncover the high quality candidates that we all want. While I agree that it is harder to uncover those candidates with solid work ethic, you can access them if you are fishing in the right ponds. Most of them are employed currently and wouldn't run across your post anyhow. Now, I do believe that posting on niche job boards is worthwhile, but even that is only a small percentage of the entire recruiting effort. We need to engage our network to its fullest extent. I regularly use e-mails, phone calls, texts, and posts on social media groups (especially niche LinkedIn groups depending on the field I am recruiting for). And think about all of the different network connections you may have from volunteering in the community, serving on boards, past job connections—the list goes on and on if you are well connected. And if you aren't well connected, then start developing that network now BEFORE you need it for recruiting others or looking for a job yourself. Leveraging your network is way more effective if you have previously and intentionally looked for ways to help your connections before you ask for something in return.

And when we get to the interview stage of the hiring process, we shouldn't forget to sell both the opportunity AND challenges/reality of the situation. If we sell the golden opportunity too much, we risk under-delivering on our promise once they realize how bad of a state the company or position is in, and if we focus solely on all of the negative reality of the situation, no one will accept our job offer in the first place. It is best to heap equal scoops of the upside potential and reality during the recruiting/ interview process.

Absence of turnover isn't the goal of the human resources function. Employee turnover should be viewed as an opportunity to make the team stronger, even if we are losing a strong team member. I have heard it said that we need to eliminate turnover. Too much turnover is definitely a problem, but having too little can be just as damaging. The right amount of turnover is highly positive; it allows new blood and ideas to enter the group. Some companies don't innovate because they are myopic and focused on their current product and market. So what is that perfect amount of turnover? The answer is that it depends. Some organizations may need a high level of turnover, others need very low, and some will need something in between. Don't take it personally when someone chooses to leave. And whatever you do, don't try to entice someone to stay. There are reasons they want to leave aside from any money, position, or benefits you can offer, and you won't make them stay in the long term by offering more money in the short term.

And don't forget; we CAN do without you. Many times I have witnessed outgoing team members who view their role as too vital for an organization to lose. And each time, it turns out that they are replaceable. Some bosses are absolutely terrified of losing key team members. I am not suggesting that we should try to lose our key employees, but as leaders we should not fear losing anyone. If that is our fear, either we do a poor job of recruiting replacement talent, or we have allowed that team member to become too critical to the organization. We have done a poor job of delegating vital responsibilities to other team members and have relied too heavily on one. This is the antithesis of team building. And by the way, this principle applies to the leader as well. We are all replaceable, including you and me. I recite this to myself and other close leaders to remind us that we are not above reproach and to stay humble about our own abilities.

True leadership is quiet and humble.

Brian Evje

Usually it is the process, not the people.[8] When we managers and leaders discover that a project is not on schedule or a product didn't get shipped or a customer service issue was handled poorly, our first instinct is usually to take it personally, get upset with the team member, and immediately, angrily tell them what they did wrong. While we certainly need to address the issue, it is our responsibility to the team member to assess the process we either intentionally or unintentionally put in place that caused the error. On occasion, it is a people problem, but that is more rare than a process issue. So assess the process first and focus your guidance of the team member on that, rather than how they personally failed. If after repeated attempts to get the person to change their behavior, they keep making the same mistakes, apply the next several sections on removing people.

Leaders are faced with many hard decisions, including balancing fairness to an individual with fairness to the group.

Robert K. Greenleaf

Sacrifice the one for the many, not the many for the one. I first heard Andy Stanley verbalize this on his monthly *Andy Stanley Leadership Podcast*. This was something I innately knew but had never put into such clear language. So many well-meaning leaders of churches, nonprofits, and even some business allow a few rotten performers spoil the whole team dynamic. Although we think we are being selfless and nice by ignoring their bad behavior, we are acting incredibly selfishly to the rest of the team. We tell ourselves we don't want to hurt this person's feelings, when we are crippling the entire team dynamic and workflow. Try to coach the problem people to better performance, but if they are rigid and don't want to change, it is selfless to the team to do the hard thing and let this person go. Confronting the issues with a poor performer is selfless, since you are doing what is right for the whole team. Hiring someone simply because they need a job isn't appropriate either, since it ultimately harms the team for the benefit of one person. If they really need a job and they are a solid fit, then by all means hire them. But let's not allow our compassion for the group to be overruled by our compassion for one.

This applies in areas related to education as well as employment. Some schools promote students to the next grade level when they are not emotionally and academically ready, which ends up hurting their classmates by slowing down the curriculum pace for those who are ready to move on to the next concept. Some parents push for their child to matriculate to the next grade level, not understanding that holding their child back is usually what's best for their child and the rest of the class. Private Christian schools have a tendency to accept a few students that have significant behavioral issues despite most private schools not being equipped to handle special needs children. This ends up causing major disruption in the classroom at the expense of the quality of education for the rest of the class. The teachers and administrators think they are being nice and helpful to the few students with issues and their parents. But it is the rest of the class that bears the brunt of the sacrifice, while school officials selfishly avoid a direct, unpleasant conversation with the parents of the problem student until much damage has been done to classmates' learning experience. The tyranny of being nice for the sake of the few must change, lest we sacrifice the many for the one.

I used to put out fires all the time. I finally figured out it was better to get rid of the arsonists.

Jay Goltz

Are you burdened by team members who don't complete their work on time, who pick fights with others, and/or are always complaining about something or someone (work or personal)? Dave Ramsey recommends you "get rid of the crazies," and I tend to agree with him. I call these people "emotionally unhealthy or unstable." Life is just too short to put up with this behavior for long. Now, I do recommend coaching problem team members to see if they can be taught how to behave and work cohesively with the team. But if after multiple meetings, you have discussed the issue openly, clearly stated what needs to change, and they still don't get it, you have an obligation to the rest of your team to remove that individual from the organization. It is important to aim to rid your organization of these people, but it's much easier if you keep them from getting hired in the first place. One of the tools I use to assess cultural fit is the Flag Page® assessment (see www.flagpage.com), but there are many other assessments that essentially do the same thing. Assessments uncover people's core motivations. When I assess potential hires, I'm not looking for any particular combination of factors, but I am looking to ferret out any emotional instability and/or cultural clashes.

Bosses should look people in the eye and show respect and compassion while delivering layoff or firing news.

@MWOnTheJob

Hire and fire moderately, not fast or slow. Many experienced executives and human resource professionals will tell you that hiring slowly and firing quickly is the ideal, while most managers follow just the opposite technique. But I feel that is an overcorrection; there should be more of a balance between the two. It is our duty as leaders to coach someone who is underperforming. At some point, however, if the team member doesn't change their behavior, the leader must act in the best interest of the whole team and remove that person. And on the hiring side of things, leaders should neither be too quick nor too slow to hire. If they hire too quickly, managers risk bringing someone on board that may not be a cultural fit or may not have the right skills. If the leader hires too slowly, the company's productivity can suffer, or the ideal candidate may be hired by another company who knows what they need and can pull the trigger more quickly.

On the night before I let someone go or fire them, I usually don't sleep. Surprisingly, I hope this never changes about me. While I don't like losing sleep, I never want to be completely comfortable with firing someone. It is a serious responsibility to hold the livelihood of another person in one's hands and choose to cut off their employment. However, I have made up my mind that I will not jeopardize the rest of the team because I can't make the decision to remove a poor performer or a divisive personality.

When it comes time to deliver the news, keep your words and explanation to a minimum; the more you talk, the more people start to think you have nefarious motives. The bottom line is that it is not about how the leader feels; it will always be harder on the team member than the manager. So don't say things like, "I know how hard this is for you" or "You will be better off" or "You will find a better job." This will sound condescending, no matter how sincere you try to be. Tell them you are deeply sorry things didn't work out and give them severance pay and benefits whether or not you have an official severance policy. Be generous to those you cut loose, but don't think they won't talk badly about you to others, even if you do the right thing. Try to let them go when the fewest team members are around to minimize the embarrassment. The team member may well get defensive and accuse you of every sort of abuse and mistreatment, but in the heat of the moment, don't go on and on about how well you've treated them. They won't understand, and in the midst of their anger or embarrassment, they will react like a wounded animal. If they approach you months or years later to tell you that they are much better off since you gave them the push, then so be it. Just don't expect gratitude; I still have people who are upset I let them go several years ago.

> You're on a need-to-know basis, and you don't need to know.

> from the movie *The Rock*

We must maintain plausible deniability for others' well-being. While some use plausible deniability as an excuse for not being transparent, I view it as not unnecessarily burdening others. Be careful what you tell your team or family members, lest you burden them with information that they don't really need to know and are unable to share with others. Some leaders will try to unburden themselves by sharing about a tough decision they had to make. This is nearly always selfish leadership. The stress and emotional weight of leadership are to be borne by leaders. So if you can't handle the pressure of having to let someone go or make some tough decision, please do us all a favor and stay a follower. The world doesn't need more managers that can't keep silent because they want to feel better emotionally. I do not advocate lying, but if you have made a particularly burdensome decision, keep it to yourself. It comes with the territory.

15

Succession Planning and Finishing Well

Success without a successor is failure

Hans Finzel, *The Top Ten Mistakes Leaders Make*

As a manager, your job is to prepare others to function sustainably without you.

@mjasmus

Teach your workers to do without you.

David Barger

According to the Family Business Institute, 97% of family businesses don't survive past the third generation.[9] This means that a lot of people who intended to leave a legacy of success and wealth to their descendants are disappointed. And whether we are part of leading a family business or working at a broader organization, we need to focus on the organization's success after we're gone. Choosing not to plan for your successor is the height of ego and selfishness. Make no mistake; whatever your excuse is for not planning, it is not valid. Not having the time or money to plan simply means you are choosing to do things other than succession planning. It is easier in the short term to focus on our own term of office. But then when we die or otherwise become impaired and can't run the organization, the organization is left in a lurch with no clear direction. Chaos is the order of the day, and many companies don't survive this stage.

Let's choose to work ourselves out of a job by training others on how to do what we do. People fear doing this because they don't want to become replaceable. Well, the good news is that you're already replaceable. If we train others how to do our job, either we will find another job with a different company or we will become an invaluable utility player for our current company. We will always be prepared for a new position in the company due to our mastery of our current role. Let's resolve to lead and plan in a way that virtually ensures organizational and relational success beyond our involvement. Continued success after our organizational participation should be our primary goal in every job we hold. Planning for that transition is one of the most selfless acts we can engage in; it says so much about the character of the leader to prepare the group for life without him. Most people understand their obligation to buy life insurance for their family in case they die. In the same way, planning for your organization's future without you is a highly caring thing to do. Start planning today if you have no plan; even if it is a basic plan, start somewhere.

Don't burn any bridges; you just never know when burning a bridge might come back to bite you in the butt.

Finish well; anyone can start well. The right reasons, the right way, and the right time: All three of these criteria should be part of any decision to leave a job, church, or other organization to ensure you don't spend your life running away from difficult situations. You may think that things will be better somewhere else, but you may be disappointed to find that the grass isn't actually greener on the other side of the fence. Sometimes difficulties come our way because we need to learn something, and that thing we need to learn will keep popping up everywhere we go. It is better to learn what we need to learn as soon as possible. This sometimes requires humbling ourselves in an area of our life that is hard to change but needs improvement. A friend of mine once told a story about not getting along with one of his brothers growing up. Let's call the brother "Mike." When my friend left home, he was so excited that he didn't have to deal with Mike anymore. But wouldn't you know it, he soon found another "Mike" in his life. This person had a different name and wasn't related but filled a similar role in my friend's life. This pattern repeated itself several times, until my friend chose to make peace with the differences and frustrations he had with his brother. After he did this, my friend never ran into another "Mike" again.

Finishing well is tough to do. We all start a new job, school, relationship, etc., with high hopes and unrealistic expectations of what we will receive from that transaction. We may overestimate the amount of money, satisfaction, power, or prestige that will accrue to us. And since we usually look at the relationship through this kind of selfish lens, we end up frustrated and looking for the exit. Now, I would like to make the case that we need to be more thoughtful about how we embark on these from the outset, but right now, I want to focus on that moment when you have decided to move on to something new.

I spent some time as a used car salesman earlier in my career, and I want to tell you a story from that time in my life to illustrate the idea of finishing well. In the car business, virtually no one gives a two-week notice. Most salesmen go from one dealership to another and tend to leave at a time when their sales are down or they are ticked at management for something. I wasn't leaving in a huff, though; I had found a new position outside of the car business and felt I should give my two weeks' notice, so I did. I found out later that during the managers' meeting, the owner asked all of the managers whether they should *allow* me to stay the last two weeks. Seems so backward, doesn't it? At any rate, they agreed I should stay and finish things. I am proud to say that I did my very best to keep my head in the game and treat customers the same way I would if I were staying. I sold several cars during the last two weeks of my tenure, and I even sold one on my last day. I am glad I was able to finish on a solid note instead of coasting.

If you have decided you want to end a business or personal relationship, please take the high road if the other party is upset that you want out. As things are coming to a close, do a better job than you did when you first started. Go the extra mile by completing all outstanding projects, leaving detailed information for your successor, and setting an example for others of how to leave. And if you happen to get enticements to stay, find a polite way to refuse them. You may be tempted by what is put on the table, but if you have decided to leave, there are probably reasons that most likely will not change.

We need to leave situations better than we found them. One of my goals in my career is to leave the organization better after my stewardship tenure than it was when I began. We should have the same goal in any relationship. As much as we might like to work with a given company or group forever, often things don't work out that way. When it's time to move on, I want to do the right thing and leave a legacy that people value. No matter how confident we are about the future, we never know when a given relationship may come to an abrupt end. We have to think about the legacy we're leaving right from the beginning. This is fresh in my mind because I recently left running one company to lead another one. I was fortunate enough to be given some feedback as I was leaving that validated the work I had put in over three and a half years. My boss said that I was the first manager in the company's nine-year history who had left things in a much healthier position than when he started. He praised my judgment in hiring professional team members, my cash-flow turnaround, and the level of professionalism I brought to the organization. I was and still am humbled by his comments and feel grateful that he recognized my commitment to the organization's continued success in setting them up for future accomplishment.

By all means, when you do leave, let it all go. Don't hold on to either the good or the bad. Have you ever known someone who has chosen to leave an organization, but then keeps calling various people in the company "just to see how things are going"? Sometimes the reality is they want to hear people talk about how awful things are now that they're gone. If they were a leader in the organization, they want to hear people criticize their replacement and say how much people want the old leader back. The ex-employee wants to hear that they are needed and that they did a much better job than the new person. This reflects a deep insecurity that does the departed employee no credit. Moreover, it handicaps the replacement, undermining his or her authority, and it causes the team to focus on the past. We should not handicap our replacements under the guise of trying to stay involved. No matter how critical we were to the company, they don't need us anymore.

The biggest emotional whiff we do when an employee departs is that we aren't happy for their move.

@TheLance

What should we do when an employee quits? First, don't give a quitting team member a counteroffer. There are almost always more important reasons why they want to leave other than money. If you give them more money and they stay, they probably won't stay for long. Second, be genuinely happy for them. As a leader, you were merely a steward of their talents while they worked for you. Consider the fact that they have completed their season of service with you, and it is time for them to move on. The organization may need the new perspective of their replacement, and the person leaving may need a new environment in order to grow professionally or personally. Take time to reflect on all of their positive contributions to the company. Bless them and thank them as they leave with all sincerity for all they have done.

16

Goals, Promises, and Optimism

Setting specific goals almost always leads to higher achievement. This was demonstrated to me by a paperclip exercise I took part in during my MBA program at Oklahoma State University. Dr. Raj Basu, one of the professors who influenced me the most, divided our class into two groups and placed us in separate rooms. He told one group to think of *as many* uses for paperclips as possible in five minutes. He separately asked the other group to think of *at least 200* uses of paperclips. Can you guess what happened? The team with the specific goal exceeded their target, coming up with over 200 uses. The other team came up with 120 or so.[10]

Organizational goals should be stretching, yet realistic. If they are too lofty and unattainable, the team is demoralized. If they are too small, attaining them is a hollow achievement. Most leaders miss the sweet spot. Either they set unrealistic goals and demoralize their team, or they set the bar too low and fail to give their team the satisfaction of meaningful achievements. There is a fine line we as leaders must walk. There is definitely an art to it, and we will get better at it the more we practice. It will help if we pay attention to things like team morale and job satisfaction. Many leaders neglect these intangibles, focusing solely on the team's achievements. Ironically, we will get more out of a team if we are in tune with how they're responding to their goals.

Sometimes arbitrary, artificial deadlines are needed in order to keep the organization from becoming too lethargic and comfortable. A deadline keeps everyone on their toes, forcing the company to achieve things sooner than they would have to otherwise. This is especially true if the workload is a bit slower than normal. Work is like a gas—it expands to fill whatever space is allotted for it. Now, if the company is working on many projects, we as leaders must be extremely careful not to abuse this principle. Don't set artificial deadlines when the team is having a hard enough time with the real ones.

We should under-promise and over-deliver on our goals/promises. We have a tendency to respond with a yes to every request without pausing to consider whether we can deliver. We think we are being polite, but by automatically saying yes, we are cheapening our word. In many cases, we won't be able to follow through on our promises. It does no good to excuse ourselves by saying that we didn't technically promise something. Whenever we say yes, we're giving our word, whether or not we use the word "promise." Even if we ultimately decide to say yes, we need to consider the time and energy required by the task and deliberately under-promise.

Before responding to a request, ask yourself these questions:

1. Conservatively, how long will this take me to complete?
2. Do I have time for this?
3. Should I even get involved in this? Does it align with my skills and strengths?

Only after carefully considering these questions should you give your answer. If you aren't able to commit to what is being asked, briefly explain why and try to find another individual that you can connect them with. If the request comes from your boss, you probably can't refuse to do it. But asking the above questions will arm you for a conversation about unrealistic expectations for the project. And remember a "no" sometimes is just "not yet"; better to not commit and delay to a time when you can deliver than to over-promise and under-deliver.

Overoptimism is more dangerous than overpessimism; it results in constant disappointment for our followers. It blinds leaders to the hazards and downsides of their decisions, usually at the expense of the organization. Sometimes the damage done is relatively harmless, but at other times it can devastate the group. I have heard those who are too optimistic say things like, "I can't believe that didn't work. I was so sure it would." Those people then repeat the same mistake over and over again. They're surprised each and every time, saying yet again, "I can't believe that didn't work. I was so sure it would." What folly, to continue to make the same mistake over and over and not recognize the need to change our actions. This doesn't give us a free pass to be overly pessimistic either, since if we were excessively cynical, we would never take risk nor try new things. Instead, try cautious optimism. Take the precaution to gather the right data about the decision or situation, but hold on to a fierce resolve that we will overcome the known and unknown obstacles we will face. The overly optimistic person chooses not to see their surroundings and sends their troops into battle (or into an ambush) without assessing and anticipating what could go wrong. Once in the heat of combat, people lose faith in their leaders, since they blindly believed things would go swimmingly easy. Let's send our troops into battle prepared and ready for whatever comes. Hope for the best and prepare for the worst.

17

Change, Decisions, and Trust

Pain is the catalyst of change.

The pain of staying the same must exceed the perceived pain of change. Because change is painful, most of us don't change until we are forced to. Many team members won't improve their behavior or productivity until they lose their job and realize how unemployable they are in their current state. Many businesses resist innovation until a competitor comes along with a new model that steals away market share. Politicians won't change until the threat of losing office looms. When the electorate gets in the mood to throw out the incumbents, it's amazing how quickly a politician can wake up and get the "religion" of change (e.g., Bill Clinton after 1994). Wisest are the leaders who anticipate what changes need to be made in their families, organizations, or relationships and take proactive, bold, measured steps in that direction. It is better to act before there is no alternative. I would much rather choose to change than be forced to change.

As iron sharpens iron, so one person sharpens another.

Proverbs 27:17, NIV

We need to foster vigorous, not vicious, debate regarding change. Robust discussion is desperately needed in today's workforce, as Patrick Lencioni so accurately depicted in *The Five Dysfunctions of a Team*. Many of us lack confidence in ourselves or the strength of our relationships, even with those closest to us personally and professionally. We tend to slink away from anything that even resembles a minor dispute. The solution is not to viciously attack others, but we should be able to be firm, direct, and fair as we advocate for our position. Leaders can cultivate vigorous discussion by hiring and retaining people who are secure enough in themselves to evaluate the worth of criticism without taking things personally. Those people are also self-effacing, introspective, and genuinely interested in improving themselves. Then we can have vigorous debate without fear of things being perceived as personal attacks. The more the team sees the leader modeling this behavior, the more comfortable they will become with this dynamic, and the more they will open up and dare others to become stronger team members.

We want neither too much nor too little change in our lives or organizations. Just like in the story of Goldilocks and the Three Bears, the sweet spot is between the two extremes. You want just the right amount of organizational change. And you want the change to happen at just the right pace; sometimes even the right amount of change causes problems because it's implemented too quickly or too slowly. Unfortunately, there is rarely a way to quantify how much change is needed or what the timing should be. This is usually learned "by feel" over time, and it is something we should be sensitive to at all times. Ask yourself and others you trust if your pace is too swift or too sluggish. This is most critical when a company is in need of a turnaround. You don't want to move too hastily and have a mutiny on your hands, but if you move too leisurely, the company can crumble around you.

So shake things up; just don't be a jerk about it. Either people are a bull in a china shop, changing things indiscriminately and without concern for others, or people never challenge the status quo out of too much concern for others' feelings. Too many companies need to be shaken; we just need leaders to do so with tact and an explanation of why things are changing. This is true in the office, home, and boardroom; sometimes, we need a person with the cojones to deftly defy the current state of affairs with thoughtfulness and sensitivity. This is what a leader does, despite how uncomfortable it might make him and others around him feel.

Indecision is the enemy of leadership, and delay is his evil twin.

There is substantial research indicating that adding more choice is helpful up to a point; then there are diminishing returns when adding too much choice actually harms the process. The harm can take the form of unnecessary postponement, vacillation, and uncertainty due to choice overload. Businesses must be careful not to give their customers more choices than are helpful. They must balance new product development with making sure the products they have in the market are high quality. Having the maximum quantity of maximum-quality products is a beautiful thing if you can achieve that delicate equilibrium. This principle also applies to internal decisions. Perhaps your business has too many options to consider, which is causing confusion and doubt. Arbitrarily whittle the list down; then it will be easier to make a decision. There are times where it is good to wait to make a choice until all the options are clear, but most of the time, even if the decision isn't urgent, we should reach a conclusion relatively quickly and move on to other important decisions. We should resist the temptation to wait for perfect information,[11] which never happens. We never get to know all of the possible chess moves, or even most of the moves, before making a decision, and trying to do so is a waste of valuable time. Life is too short to allow ourselves to get stuck on any one choice, no matter how important it may seem.

Making clear, unambiguous, collective decisions and setting distinct direction is a critical but difficult role in leadership. We think we're being nice by allowing people lots of freedom in their work, but it actually creates more chaos. I don't want to say anything against freedom, but there is something to be said for the security and stability that people feel when their work has boundaries. People actually crave these kinds of boundaries at work. This is not an excuse to micromanage people, but we must clearly define for them what the organization stands for and what it won't tolerate. People yearn for clarity, but most of the time their leaders give them obscurity. Perhaps we are unsure where to draw a hard line on certain issues or are afraid we will send a message of distrust by clearly delineating what we want them to do (and more importantly, what we don't want them to do). A friend of mine suggested I use the Start/Stop/Continue method when setting direction for team members. You simply tell someone what they need to start, stop, and continue doing, which immediately removes ambiguity. Those who report to us genuinely desire to have role and rule clarity; we owe it to them to elucidate things in a respectful but direct manner.

As leaders we are wired to come to conclusions, but the

temptation is to make them individually, not collectively, which causes us to lose sight of the big picture. Many smaller organizations routinely mess this up because they don't even have annual budgeting and strategic plans. Let's get out of the minutiae and fly up to 30,000 feet before we give our okay on a project. Admittedly, this gets harder and harder the larger our organizations become, since the leaders tend to get further and further away from what is happening on the front lines. At times, we do need to make decisions on the fly, but it should be rare. If it becomes too frequent, we risk losing sight of the big picture and could make a decision that is 180 degrees counter to the overall, ideal strategy to execute. Balance making individual decisions in a vacuum during crisis with making collective decisions for longer-term planning. Truthfully, this is a delicate balance, but focusing on longer-term decisions is worth the extra energy and effort.

You attract more flies with honey than with vinegar.

Explain your decision and others will follow, even if they disagree. Too often, we want people to follow us simply because we are in charge. But this is a very selfish and dictatorial way of looking at things. It's the old style of management that most of our parents and grandparents experienced in the workplace. In an earlier time, it worked quite well, emerging out of the American military experience in two World Wars. But that top-down method of management is crumbling. Generation X, Y, and Z aren't used to this style at all, and most reject it in favor of a more collaborative, team-centered approach. They want leaders who will humble themselves and earn their trust; they won't automatically give it. "Old-school" managers should take heed of this generational shift lest they find them-selves prematurely unemployed one day.

Explaining our decisions to the team is not an act of weakness, as some might think. It is just the opposite; it is a sign of strength and conviction about the decision that the leader would choose to expose himself to poten-tial criticism. The weak leader is the one who refuses to explain his decisions because he takes all criticism person-ally. The dirty little secret is that our team members *will* criticize our decisions behind our back, especially if we don't explain them. But if we take the time to elucidate things, our team members still may not agree, but most will follow anyway. The little courtesy, respect, and humility that you show them by explaining yourself will go a long way.

Leaders have faith in people. They believe in them. They have found that others will rise to high expecta-tions.

Robert K. Greenleaf

Being direct and setting expectations isn't being mean. True leadership clearly communicates expectations and holds people accountable. Wimpy leadership does neither. Believe it or not, the type of team members you want to retain desire clear communication about what you expect of them and their work. You may have a team member that you have allowed to consistently miss deadlines. Or perhaps you implied you would set up a bonus structure and never did. People don't like too much ambiguity. Not knowing where they stand makes them anxious and unhappy. Leaving some expectations unspoken is normal for any business; you don't want to treat your team members like reckless teenagers. Be careful not to get lazy about communication. If you don't talk about expectations until a major problem surfaces, you have no excuse to fly off the handle and shout at your team members for not delivering something they didn't know was an expectation of their position.

Setting clear and definitive expectations from the start doesn't take much effort and can forestall many problems. This is why writing agreements, even if simply in an e-mail, is so important. Most people avoid putting agreements in writing because they don't want to take the time to definitively spell out terms. They prefer ambiguity, since it gives them more room to maneuver in their attempt to win at the other person's expense. A written agreement makes it harder to take advantage of your partner, but it does make it easier to look for the "win-win" (as Stephen Covey taught us to do in *Seven Habits of Highly Effective People*). Another advantage of putting our intentions in writing is that we're forced to make more conservative projections, since we know that we're more accountable for what we put in writing. If we are continually setting expectations off the cuff, we may paint too rosy of picture. Initially, team members are energized by all of the grandiose ideas and promises of impressive things to come. However, once they realize these vague guarantees are mostly hollow, they lose faith in our leadership.

Know when to ask for input or give direction without input. There is a time for getting someone's input and a time to be direct in telling them what you require of them. But we often use more passive than direct language. For some reason, we feel more comfortable with "Please, would you, could you do this," and it is just plain wishy-washy. It is also important to use more declarative and less open-ended "asks" of others we lead. We should use less "would you's" and "could you's", and instead try more "here's what I need you to do's". We can still be polite while directing someone to do something.

If I can't trust a person to do this, then I need a different person.

Bob Iger

You either trust someone or you don't. So recognize when you don't trust a person, and do something about it. This one trips up a lot of managers, since we tend to put up with lack of accountability from a team member until we just can't stand them anymore. We will say things like "I am so frustrated with Bob. He didn't follow through on a project for the umpteenth time." If you don't trust someone, then do something about it. Talk to the person and reiterate what the expectations are; then allow them to experience the natural consequences of their actions. And if they won't listen after repeated discussion and consequences, don't keep banging your head against the wall; let them go. Don't prolong the agony for them or yourself.

People do what you inspect, not what you expect.

Louis Gerstner

Trust but verify. We often choose not to inspect the work of someone under our leadership in order to avoid the dreaded label of "micromanager." While we have all run into a few true micromanagers, holding others accountable by periodically inspecting and giving input to their work is not necessarily micromanagement if done in a constructive, professional manner. It is simply a way to reinforce the company's ethos. In the absence of verification, customer service, quality, and consistency are left completely up to individuals who each have different methods. This can create an inconsistent brand message to your customers, and having consistent methods and procedures, our customers can count on the service they receive each time, similar to what we all experience when we visit McDonald's stores in various different locations.

18

Correction, Accountability, and Teachable Moments

The buck stops here.

Harry Truman

Mutual responsibility is at the core of accountability; the onus is not solely on the manager to provide direction. It is equally the duty of the leader and team member to hold each other accountable. There are things the leader must provide and other things the team member must provide. The former needs to provide the resources and clear expectations for the team member to do their job, and the latter must be accountable for doing quality and timely work. Jim Hunter, an author and speaker on Servant Leadership, explains accountability this way: "You need to do a little hugging and a little spanking with your team members" (figuratively, of course). If someone needs to be held accountable for some action taken or not taken, then we should welcome that, since it will only serve to make the team that much stronger. We should encourage them and bring correction to areas that need improvement. One without the other shows that we don't care as leaders. To do both in a kind and professional manner is what we signed up for when we assumed the role of a leader. Holding people accountable should start with looking at ourselves in the mirror. Too often we like to point out the faults of team members before we take steps to change our own behavior. Team members will more readily accept your oversight and input if they see you holding yourself to a higher standard. I even recommend charging trustworthy team members with holding you accountable for anything you can't complete in less than a few days.

As leaders, we have a responsibility to correct and motivate those entrusted to our stewardship. A manager is responsible for his people, not the human resources department. If something needs to be discussed with a team member, it is the manager's responsibility, not that of human resources, to address the issue with the team member. So often managers don't want to do the hard part of their job and instead want an HR person to deliver the corrective message to the team member. We are all responsible for those who work directly and indirectly for us. Let's not pass the buck to the HR department; they are busy enough.

I have heard it said that you can't correct someone if you didn't witness the incident firsthand; this is ludicrous! Someone is living in Alice's Wonderland. If we followed that prescription literally, there would be all kinds of issues going unaddressed in most companies. With that said, we must be wise and discerning to know whom we should depend on to give us secondhand information and to whom we should delegate to handle the situation. Some employees have ulterior, selfish motives, and others are outright liars. We should rely on trustworthy individuals to relay areas the organization should improve. This must be done delicately so as to not turn certain honorable people into "narcs." But if you get rid of the offenders who repeatedly make the same mistakes, the stronger team members will welcome those who hold the team accountable.

And be careful not to rush to judgment, especially with only one source of information. There are exceptions to this rule—for example, if the source has proven their reliability many times over many years. But for the most part, human nature wants to rush to judgment with the first witness's testimony. This is dangerous, since you haven't verified the accusation or given the accused the ability to respond in a nonthreatening dialogue. So get the facts from two or more witnesses, and then allow both affected team members to give you their account of what happened. Ask neutral questions without negative body language or tone of voice. For example, you could say, "Tell me about this project and what went wrong from your perspective." Our posture should be one of information gathering, not blame assignation.

If we overreact when people make mistakes in our organization, we often enact systems designed to detect those types of mistakes. So we end up with multiple people triple-checking everything, rather than getting to the root cause and removing the problem person or changing the process. What we don't realize is that this path is counterproductive, since it focuses on detection rather than prevention. Let's choose to focus on prevention instead. Rather than waste time, energy, and effort to detect the next mistake, we should channel our effort into systems and people that prevent issues in the future, all the while fully accepting the fact that no system will prevent all mistakes.

You treat people well, they will return the favor. And if

you treat them poorly, they will return the favor.

Mike Sheehan

Major on the majors; minor on the minors. We have all had a boss, parent, or other superior who has meted out punishment or correction that didn't fit the crime. If the issue is major in nature, then by all means take corrective action that reflects that. But people lose all respect and trust in us as leaders the moment we major on a minor issue. They instinctively know when they or someone else has been unfairly assessed or chastised. The root of this issue is that we take small things personally and fly off the handle on every minor issue. If we are judicious in making wise choices, others will naturally respect us. They will follow us because they want to, not because they have to. They will even go the extra mile for us because they have confidence that we will not sweat the small stuff.

Lack of planning on your part does not constitute an emergency on mine.

Many of us have seen this motto up on the wall in some office or school. I'm not sure who came up with it, but I first saw it on the door of my music composition professor, Dr. Jerry Hatley.[12] Simply put, we owe it to others to plan ahead. Blaming them for not bailing us out at the last minute is selfish and illogical. A common excuse I hear is, "I didn't have time to complete this because I ran into this unanticipated delay," or some variation thereof. I recognize that we can't anticipate everything, but we need to proactively anticipate more of those potential delays; this is the part of accountability that we as team members need to embrace. We don't get to complain about the delays in our project, whether legitimate or illegitimate. We should build sufficient additional time into our schedule to allow for truly unanticipated delays.

There are always natural consequences to our actions whether we notice them or not, and we tend to learn best if we have to bear the natural consequences of our actions. For example, if I choose to tick off my boss enough times, most likely he will fire me. If I run out into the middle of a busy street, I am most likely going to hit by a car and thus suffer the physical consequences of that unwise decision. As leaders, we are often tempted to protect our team members from various natural consequences. Perhaps someone didn't fill out a form that you asked them to, and you know that failure will cause the business harm. We usually go fill out the form ourselves. Withholding natural consequences is an act of selfishness that fixes the short-term problem, but we have just created a much bigger long-term issue. If we had allowed the natural consequences to fall on that team member, the business would have been negatively affected in the short run, but the team member would have learned a valuable lesson in how their actions affect others in the long run. We should coach our team members in a way that points out how to minimize negative consequences of their actions, but we must remember that consequences cannot be avoided outright. To think we can preempt all team member mistakes is naïve and detrimental to the learning of others around us. After we have done our part as leaders by coaching, we must step back and allow others the opportunity to make mistakes, even if it costs us or the company something of value in the short term.

People often say motivation doesn't last. Neither

MILES ANTHONY SMITH

does bathing—that's why we recommend it daily.

Zig Ziglar

As a father, husband, friend, volunteer, and leader at work, it is my duty to look for opportunities to teach and coach others that I have stewardship over. As I earn the right to speak into their lives, I need to be sensitive to openings to interject wisdom at times that feel natural, not forced. It should flow freely into the conversation, and if I have to force it, the other person probably won't receive the advice I am trying to impart. As parents, we often do a bad job at this; life passes by so quickly and we don't seize the occasions when our kids are young to prepare them for life. Then when they become teenagers, we panic and try to influence their behavior; usually they reject this, since they intuitively recognize that we didn't earn their trust early on. Now, teenagers aren't always going to listen, even if we have been intentionally looking for teachable moments all their lives. However, even if they appear to ignore us, they do hear us if we spent the time to earn their trust from an early age. By the time they are teenagers their habits and morals are mostly set, so it behooves us to get started early. We have a similar responsibility toward those who work for us; we need to look for times where we can convey important insight about leadership. The sooner we start developing this habit, the sooner team members learn to expect and value it. Coaching others proves we care about them enough to develop them beyond just their career with XYZ Company.

Providing feedback to individual team members can be a great opportunity for teaching the entire team. But the proper way to do this is in most cases is to praise publicly and coach privately. A number of leaders have this backward; they berate and shame team members publicly, humiliating them in front of their peers and thinking that shame will motivate them to change their behavior, which results in cover-up rather than freely admitting mistakes. Bosses usually completely neglect to praise their team at all, let alone in public. When we praise people publicly, it reinforces the positive behavior to the group and signals to the praised that they are valued. Coaching or correcting in private shows that you respect yourself, the team, and the offender enough to gently and firmly ask them to change their actions next time. The only exception is if someone is publicly disobedient or inappropriate. Then it must be addressed immediately and in public in a fair but firm manner. This team member opened themselves up to public correction when they chose to disobey or act inappropriately in front of everyone.

19

Wrap-up

Putting the needs of our organizations first is painful, but necessary. We owe it to the time to hire the right fit and fire the wrong fit, but we should be careful not to allow the end to justify the means, wrongly applying the mantra "Sacrifice the one for the many." Lopping off the heads of people whose personality conflicts with ours and replacing them with a horde of mini-me's is inexcusable. We should recognize we are responsible for necessary organizational change, swift decision-making abilities, and accountability through coaching, which cuts both ways between team member and leader. A manager isn't merely supposed to tell everyone else what to do and how they are doing it wrong. Leaders must look for teachable moments with others but remain humble themselves to allow others to gently point out their own areas of weakness.

PART 3

Humility 101: Authentic Authority

It is quite risky to let our guard down and make ourselves vulnerable with others by giving them the right—no, the duty—to call us out on our faults. But doing so allows us to prove our true leadership in the sense that we are comfortable in who we are, despite our shortcomings and insecurity. This leads to others recognizing and choosing to follow our trustworthy, genuine authority.

20

Apologies, Authority,
and At Ease

Selfish apologies aren't apologies at all. Do you say things like "I'm sorry you feel that way," or "I'm sorry, but my intentions were good," or "I'm sorry, but I can't help it," or "I'm sorry you took it that way," or "I'm sorry I made a mistake, but ...."? If so, please stop it. This kind of behavior is purely selfish; it reveals that we are trying to make ourselves feel better for our poor performance. We are not offering a sincere apology. Instead, say things like "I'm sorry. I was wrong, and I will do endeavor to do better next time." Then actually work on doing better next time. None of us are perfect, but people can tell the difference between a failure by someone who is genuinely trying to get better and a failure by someone who is not trying. Don't offer any excuses; the minute you do, you invalidate your apology. Your relationship with your boss, co-workers, spouse, kids, etc., will be much healthier and filled with mutual trust and respect if you create a habit of genuine apologies. Another apology that is rather selfish is "I am sorry for any inconvenience this may have caused." ANY inconvenience? No, it should be THE inconvenience we have caused. This one takes place in business often, and is a way to weasel out of an actual admission of failure. So let's apologize for THE inconvenience we caused and promise to do better next time, regardless of whether it was truly our fault.

107

The circumstances of life, events of life, and people in life do not make me the way I am but reveal the way I am.

Dr. Sam Peeples

Bad experiences made me a better boss. The worst moments in our career often teach us the most.

Ruth J. Simmons

Being a strong leader even if we follow an insecure leader is a hard one to swallow. Having a boss who reacts out of insecurity is equally alarming and disconcerting. However, it is not an excuse to be the same unassured, weak leader ourselves. We owe it to our team members and family to treat them with the level of respect we wish our boss would give us. We must choose to die to self and give others what we are not getting from our leader. This breaks the cycle of poor leadership that can otherwise infect the entire organization. I'm not saying that if we find ourselves following a weak leader, we have an obligation to stay there forever. While we are faithfully leading, we can look for another situation with a leader we want to emulate. We should not use the fact that we work for a weak leader to be an excuse to abuse people who follow us.

I have learned so much about leadership by observing other leaders' poor decisions and habits, sometimes more than I care to. I then must choose to be a better leader for others than what was modeled for me. While it is frustrating to see other managers leading in a selfish manner, we must choose to do the opposite of what we see from their poor leadership. Rather than be dismayed by bad leadership, pursue the opportunity to learn how not to do things. We should allow it to deepen our resolve to be a better leader and not frustrate our followers. I can attest that this is a struggle for me, and I know it isn't easy. But it is the right thing to do to develop our leadership ability. We must humble ourselves if we are to become stronger leaders.

> When Jesus returned to Capernaum, a Roman officer came and pleaded with him, "Lord, my young servant lies in bed, paralyzed and in terrible pain." Jesus said, "I will come and heal him." But the officer said, "Lord, I am not worthy to have you come into my home. Just say the word from where you are, and my servant will be healed. I know this because I am under the authority of my superior officers, and I have authority over my soldiers. I only need to say, 'Go,' and they go, or 'Come,' and they come. And if I say to my slaves, 'Do this,' they do it." When Jesus heard this, he was amazed. Turning to those who were following him, he said, "I tell you the truth, I haven't seen faith like this in all Israel!"

> Matthew 8:5-10, NLT

What an incredible story about a high ranking leader that cared enough about his servant to help him get well. As a Roman officer, this man didn't have to serve his servant, but he chose to. He understood that true authority comes from being under authority and recognized that Jesus was one who had authority. Many people do not understand or accept the need for an organizational structure. Most would rather bypass the established hierarchy and go over someone's head. I have had several occasions where an indirect report will start to talk to me about an issue with their direct manager. I stop them before they even get started and ask if they have addressed it with their direct manager yet. I almost universally hear, "Um, no." I ask them to speak with their direct manager and then come back to talk to me if their issue is still not addressed at that point.

A great leader has learned first how to be a great follower and one who has a respect for leadership structure. Leaders don't allow others to routinely circumvent the normal chain of command. It only causes confusion and dysfunction and undermines other mid-level leaders. Some think that getting to that level where they don't have to report to anyone is the ultimate goal of life, but authority cannot exist without sincere accountability. We are fooling ourselves at best and believing a lie at worst. There's a word for thinking that we don't have to answer to anybody: hubris. We will always be under authority, and thinking otherwise can lead to a downfall. Even if we are the owner or chairman of the board, we still need someone else to hold us accountable. We can only be in true authority if we are subject to another's authority.

Act like you have the authority, but do not reach for the power.

Os Hillman

Be different. Be understated; allow others to underestimate you. I personally relish the fact that people underrate me, since I have the chance to exceed their expectations nearly every time. So many people overstate their qualifications that if we do the opposite, we will stand out. Some will hate us for it or be jealous of the attention. But that's okay. Don't reach for power; earn influence with others. Most people aren't expecting low-key leaders who don't need the limelight. Choose to be remarkable, no matter what others think or say about you. I use "remarkable" in Seth Godin's sense of something people find worth remarking about. Being understated is so rare in our media-frenzied, over-the-top culture; what we really need are leaders with an unassuming yet powerful behind-the-scenes style.

The secret to positioning is to simply make whatever's different about you your strength.

Craig Garber

Are you comfortable in your own skin? Becoming comfortable in one's own skin requires not fearing others' perception of oneself; it is a choice not to let fear of what others think determine our course. Most of us are concerned about what others believe about us. It's part of our human nature. It is a matter of choice and force of will not to let the fear of man direct or divert our path unnecessarily. It takes time to be at ease with yourself; many of us take decades to come to a place of confidence in who we are, despite our imperfections. Once you reach this place, others can sense it; they know that you choose not to let the fear of others sway you. If you struggle in this area, remember that we are all weird in some way, and since no one is perfect, there is a peace in knowing who you are and not trying to be something you are not. We do need to imitate others' good habits, but we must take those and make them our own so that we remain authentic. People can sense when you are trying too hard to be exactly like someone else.

111

In Seth Godin's book *We Are All Weird,* he encourages us not to be afraid of being unconventional, since non-conformity is what makes life interesting. Here's how I'm weird. I have two seemingly incompatible degrees: a Bachelor's degree in Music Composition and a Master's degree in Business Administration. I was the only one in any of my MBA classes who had a music background. For me, this seeming incongruity is a wonderful, unique perspective that not many other business leaders have, one that lends a wealth of creativity, particularly in the area of marketing. I consider my own weirdness a blessing, since it differentiates me from my peers in a positive way. As I have become more secure in how I am different from the masses, my confidence level has soared. I needn't worry about what people think, since I know my primary responsibility is to live my life according to how God has wired me.

21

Capability of Culpability

Avoid the caustic culture of celebrity, and don't idolize leaders. At many times during history, cultures have adored vaunted celebrities. From the warriors of ancient Greece and Rome to the present-day celebrities of Hollywood, human nature desires to put certain types of people on a pedestal and idolize them. Unfortunately, in doing so, we miss the fact that those celebrities are just like us; they have bad days and make mistakes. They are, after all, still human and not the gods we suppose them to be. This illusion of celebrity that pervades our culture today is highly caustic to an unwitting public. Most people strive to become famous, since they hold famous people in such high regard. Then they are either disappointed that they never achieved that status, or if they do become a celebrity, they find that it is empty in the end. It fulfills no purpose in life and brings no true happiness. What we miss is the fact that selfless and obscure living is highly rewarding and gives us a sense of purpose that satisfies our soul much more than celebrity ever could.

Rather than idolize leaders we think of highly, we should view both their strengths and weaknesses, recognizing that even those who look perfect aren't. Then we should aim to emulate their good habits and shun the bad ones. If we allow ourselves to buy into the myth that celebrity leaders are perfect and without blame, we do ourselves and society a great injustice. We believe a lie that has never been and never will be true. And I can speak from experience; I have watched many a leader fall that I held up as my ideal. Over and over, I would be disappointed and crushed; fortunately, I never fell prey to the disillusionment that befalls so many. Watching these leaders make public mistakes only deepened my resolve to be a better leader and purposefully surround myself with people who would assuredly keep me accountable.

When I was in college, I went to a church that was one of the fastest growing churches in the U.S. at the time. They were even featured on the cover of a major Christian magazine. The pastor was an amazing leader, highly regarded by the church and the community. But then it was discovered that he was having an affair, and things unraveled at the church. Many people became disillusioned with every church and every pastor. Just as I was reeling from this scandal, I saw another hero of mine, a pastor from a previous church, on the six o'clock news. He had been busted by a police sting for solicitation of prostitution. The reporter shoved a camera and microphone in his face, asking him what his wife would do once she found out. Needless to say, he was speechless.

Fortunately, even after both of these traumatic events, I didn't lose faith in every leader. But I learned a valuable lesson not to put absolute faith in any one person. It simply sets them up for failure and sets us up for disappointment when they make a mistake. Having said that, we do need leaders who will stand up and choose to do what is right, but leaders are human and all of them will make poor choices. Some of them will fail spectacularly. And even though leaders have failed me, I won't stop trusting all leaders, just the ones who prove untrustworthy.

I should mention that both of the pastors I refer to have confessed their mistakes and turned from their moral failings. As far as I know, they are now making right moral choices. I commend them for this and believe that they have both had an authentic transformation. Humbling ourselves when we make mistakes and choosing not to repeat those mistakes re-qualifies us for leadership.

Sudden elevation frequently leads to pride and a fall. The most exacting test is to survive prosperity.

John Oswald Sanders

Nearly all men can stand adversity, but if you want to test a man's character, give him power.

Abraham Lincoln

Prosperity and power are harder to handle than we realize. In our culture, obsessed with greed, fame, and celebrity, it is particularly hard to believe that prosperity is harder to handle than adversity. We have elevated power and fame as the top goals of life, but I can assure you that they are unable to bring joy or happiness to our lives. It is no small feat not to be crushed under the weight of prosperity and power. This is counterintuitive to us, since we believe instinctively that if we just had more money and power, our lives would be better, since we would have more control. Yet in practice, things are usually harder with more money and power, since you are responsible for more. You have more decisions to make about how to spend money and how to wield power and authority. Keep this in mind when you pine for more cash and influence than you have. Perhaps you don't have more because you can't handle more.

Success yesterday is no guarantee of success tomorrow.

With success, refuse to believe your own press. Surrounding yourself with genuinely humble people will help guard against believing your own press. You have to start this habit long before you become successful. If you don't start early in your career, and you end up with success, it will be nearly impossible to see your own hubris. Many leaders have failed spectacularly in this area, especially as success breeds more success, and accolades from other leaders, companies, and media outlets blind them to their personal and professional weaknesses, not to mention the incestuous inner circle of "yes men" that affirm the leader and shield them from negative criticism. Cultivate and train yourself to be suspicious of your own motives and beware of your own rationalizations. Self-awareness in this area takes intentional and consistent practice.

The worst sin of a CEO is not greed but pride.

Dr. Jeffrey Gandz

While none of us wants to make mistakes, I would much rather be an easily correctable fool than someone who blindly refuses to accept responsibility for errors and is strong-willed to a fault. It is important to give trustworthy people permission and opportunity to bust you. If you don't regularly remind your trusted and closest advisors that they have permission and duty to professionally and privately point out your mistakes or weakness, they just won't do it. Charging key, trusted team members with giving you feedback will work only if you regularly solicit feedback from them on specific projects or actions. The more frequently this happens, the more comfortable your team members will feel in privately and professionally calling you out. I try to hire people around me who will tell me the truth, thus hopefully helping me avoid failures in my life or business. Giving them the opportunity is equally important. It can be as simple as routinely asking for feedback, either at the end of each project or at regular intervals (e.g., once a month). We must let those closest to us know that we are not intimidated by private and professional criticism. Then we must not abuse our critics by lashing out at their genuine attempts to show us our blind spots. If we will react and take their criticism personally, then we might as well not give them permission and authority to hold up the mirror for us to see. This takes being secure and comfortable in our own skin, knowing who we are, who we are not, and being at peace with our shortcomings and strengths.

Be sure that your sin will find you out.

Numbers 32:23, NLT

Character is the ability to carry out a good resolution long after the excitement of the moment has passed.

Cavett Robert

Human nature tends to believe that there are superhuman leaders who are to be revered for their godlike ability to not make mistakes. Well, I have news for you: No one is completely without fault. Even the pope isn't infallible in this sense! I'm not trying to pick a fight about doctrine, I'm just pointing out that even according to official Roman

Catholic teaching, the pope isn't immune from sin, faults, and mistakes. So no matter how much you admire a particular leader, don't neglect to weigh whether what they're teaching and modeling is worth accepting.

Regrettably, it is a myth that enough experience and wisdom can somehow make us immune to immorality, but character requires constant development. Many of us want desperately to believe this myth. Just think about all of the leaders you have known (either in your own world or who are public leaders) who have made major moral mistakes. I can think of far too many. Congressman Anthony Weiner, President Bill Clinton, and Pastor Ted Haggard were people who seemingly had it all and made poor decisions that risked losing it all. We must work on our character each and every day if we are to stand tall as leaders and not let others down. We must be relentless in our own character development.

When facing a tough decision, ask yourself whether you would regret doing it more than not doing it.

We must anticipate ethical dilemmas and set our mind like concrete if we are to avoid making unethical decisions. If we don't foresee ethical dilemmas, we will routinely find ourselves in situations where we risk not making the ethical choice. And there is a difference between what is technically legal and what is ethical. The histories of Enron, Global Crossing, MCI WorldCom, and others are replete with examples of poor ethical decisions, not just poor legal decisions. I would be willing to bet that most, if not all, of those executives had never thought through beforehand how they would act in the ethical dilemma that ultimately ended their career. We must aim to predict those situations as best we can and think through how we should deal with them. Making our choice and setting our mind like stone when we aren't pressured or stressed will make it easier to do the right thing in the heat of the moment.

Conflicts of interest are an area where we can have ethical dilemmas. The secret to diffusing conflicts of interest is to acknowledge and communicate them up front. If conflicts of interest are dealt with before they arise, people rarely have a problem with them. Publicly acknowledging your interests gives you the opportunity to address the issue and set expectations to avoid the appearance of malfeasance. The danger is when things are not disclosed and problems arise later; then people feel betrayed and lied to.

22

Authenticity Deficit Disorder

Authenticity is doing what you promise, not "being who you are."

Seth Godin

If authenticity is as Seth defines, then we have a dearth of authenticity in our world today. We routinely make promises every day that we either have no intention of following through or do not consider to be promises. We don't have an *attention* deficit disorder pandemic but rather an *authenticity* deficit disorder one. If we don't recognize this and take action to consider our commitments more carefully and follow through on those commitments, younger generations that follow and look up to us will reject and distrust our leadership.

Rarely do we keep our word if it will cost us, but we should always keep our word . . . especially when it costs us. We are so concerned about our short-term interest (time, money, reputation, etc.) that we lose sight of the long-term trust that will be gained by sticking to our promises. What if your promise will cost you your job or will cause your house to go into foreclosure? Or what if it will cause you to lose your professional license or something else of great value? We all have a price above which we will sacrifice our integrity; my challenge to you

121

is to break that barrier, choosing to never sacrifice your integrity no matter the consequences. Your word, and by extension your name and reputation, is worth far more than money or time.

No plan is worth the paper it is printed on unless it starts doing. There is too much telling in this life and not enough doing.

William H. Danforth

We desperately need leaders who will guide us with less talk and more action. Please show us; don't tell us. God knows we have enough of the opposite. Put another way, "Ignore what people say, watch what they do." This applies in relationships as well as in companies. How often do dating couples tell each other they love each other, yet their selfish actions prove otherwise. Have you ever had someone apologize for an action, and then turn right around and behave the same way? It is no longer enough to say something if we won't follow through on our word. When my children approach dating age, I will endeavor to instill this in them, so they can avoid the kind of flaky people who don't honor their word. Mean what you say, and say what you mean. It is rather simple to explain yet so hard to practice consistently.

Another application of this principle is to take time now and then to get your hands dirty at work. Lend help in some area of your organization that involves manual labor or other low-status work. You will prove to others that you are committed to the vision when you roll up your sleeves and get dirty. When people see that you are not above doing any job, they rally behind you. If you get this right, it will breed a fierce loyalty in people that cannot be coerced, controlled, or managed any other way.

When I see an unresolved issue, I jump in. When I'm walking around campus, if there's trash, I pick it up.

Jack Dangermond

We need more substance over style, since we have a plethora of the opposite in our culture. Flashy looks good on the surface, but a flashy mask is probably covering up a lot of warts. Without deep and substantive leadership, the best-case scenario is that nothing gets done. At worst, lies are told as to what is being done and/or what the real problems are. The world needs more outwardly boring, mundane leaders that get things accomplished and speak with integrity about the problems facing the organizations they are leading. The time has come for transparent leaders who choose substance over style; forget the upcoming election or whatever other threat looms. Let's choose to do the right thing for the organization and put ourselves in harm's way if necessary.

Build icebergs, not skyscrapers. The foolish are continually busy building an edifice above the surface, while the wise are building below the surface where no one can see. You may have seen the artist's image of an iceberg with 90% of it below the water's surface. You can't see it normally, but what lies below has an enormous impact. Just ask the captain of the RMS *Titanic*. We would often rather build something much more noticeable (a skyscraper) because we want to wow others with our outward accomplishments. But what we build for others to notice is usually a façade covering a shaky foundation. With the passage of time, others will be able to see past the façade to the reality of both strategies. Eventually, many will marvel at the wise person's accomplishments as if they just happened overnight. They will see the creaking, crumbling construction of the foolish for what it is—but only after much time has passed. The wise instinctively know that it is better to build things out of view and then execute their plans with surprising accuracy. The foolish want to be noticed the instant they accomplish anything.

Be Chris LeDoux, not Garth Brooks. Now, don't get me wrong, Garth is one of my favorite country singers; he even happens to have graduated from one of the same schools I did (Go Pokes!). But do you know who Chris LeDoux is? If you have heard of him, it's probably a direct result of the impact he had on Garth Brooks's musical career. Garth mentions him as his inspiration in several of his songs and in many interviews. Chris LeDoux had a relatively obscure career as a country musician and rodeo competitor. Let's not forget the lesson here—we can have a much stronger impact from a position of relative obscurity. I want to be the kind of person that enables other leaders to start at my level and achieve even greater things than I. And make no mistake; I have set a high standard for my own success. Let's all strive for that ideal of encouraging and pushing others to greater success than our own, and the world will be a better place.

Be a forecaster, not a reporter. Forecast and foresee future business trends based on real-time data; don't be the person who simply brings the data to their boss like a dog brings a newspaper to his master. Bring your analysis/forecast to your leader, and you will be invaluable to your company team. Reporter types can be much more easily fired or let go when budget cuts are necessary, but forecasters are almost never fired. Don't simply do the minimum job you think you can get away with; look for ways to anticipate things that are on the horizon and advise your boss as to how best to position the company to take advantage of that future.

23

Adversity Isn't to Be Avoided: Struggle Well

The pathway to leadership almost always takes us through the valley of adversity.

Os Hillman

Some of the hardest yet most fulfilling times in my life have come during times of significant challenge. Most of us endeavor to avoid difficult times like the bubonic plague, but adversity wreaks enormous growth and enables us to succeed at a higher level than most. The few who understand this are the ones who achieve the most. So don't fight it; even though I admit it is hard not to. I would not choose to go back and relive the toughest times in my life, but I absolutely wouldn't trade them for all the riches in the world. Something changes in us if we submit to adverse times and learn what we need from them to help us on our journey in the future. Much as gold is refined in the fire to burn off impurities, so we must be refined through the fire of hardship.

We are pressed on every side by troubles, but we are not crushed. We are perplexed, but not driven to despair. We are hunted down, but never abandoned by God. We get knocked down, but we are not destroyed. Through suffering, our bodies continue to share in the death of Jesus so that the life of Jesus may also be seen in our bodies.

2 Corinthians 4:8-10, NLT

We have three responses to adversity or suffering: Resistance, Resignation, or Submission. And since resistance is futile (as the Borg taught us), that path will only result in frustration and hardening our heart towards others. Resignation is usually what I gravitate toward; I know there isn't much I can do given certain circumstances that I cannot control. So I throw my hands in the air and allow depression to overtake me. But the wisest path is submission. Submission doesn't mean mere passivity or pretending that everything's okay. It means that we embrace the challenging times and seek to learn from them and find true joy in spite of the circumstances. It is the simple kindness or generosity that others show during these times that mean the most. But if our heart is focused on resistance or resignation, we rob ourselves of the small joys and wins during the storm in our lives. Choose submission, and you will learn much and understand genuine happiness despite tough times.

What do you do when you've done all you can, and it seems like it's never enough? And what do you say when your friends turn away, and you're all alone, alone? Tell me, what do you give when you've given your all, and it seems like you can't make it through? Well you just stand when there's nothing left to do. You just stand; watch the Lord see you through. Yes, after you done all you can, you just stand.

Donnie McClurkin, "Stand"

I first heard this song when I was in high school. I was going through a tough time battling depression. The song encouraged my soul and gave me the courage to stand in the midst of challenging times. I just knew I couldn't give up; I had to hang in there no matter how bad things got. It is true that after we have done all we can, sometimes we just have to choose to stand, hanging in there and choosing to believe that things will get better, even when we don't know how long that will take. Choosing resolve over capitulation in spite of tough times will only make us stronger and deepen our leadership character and ability. So after you've done all you can, just stand.

It's the character that's the strongest that God gives the most challenges to. Now you can take that as a compliment.

from the movie *Return to Me*

As humans, we are born with this innate desire to live in a sort of paradise or utopia where there is eternal peace and harmony among all peoples. The problem is that we live in a fallen world filled with sin and pain, and our role is to learn to live a fulfilled life, not a happy one. True happiness can only come from selfless leadership. So we must struggle well, since we will have trouble in this life. Life is an epic struggle, and it takes a valiant, unswerving, daily effort to be consistently successful in the various arenas of life (faith, family, friends, business, etc.). This is true no matter how much or how little money, power, and influence you

129

have, so don't believe the myth that if you just have more of those things that life will be easier. Life is lived well when we learn to "struggle well"; we learn how to learn from our missteps. We seek out and seize opportunities to learn how to be a better spouse, parent, friend, businessperson, etc.

While we don't like to struggle ourselves, we definitely don't like to watch others suffer. But we must neither exploit nor supplant the adversity or pain of others, lest we delay positive growth. You probably have heard the story of a man who assisted a caterpillar's extrication from its cocoon, only to watch the newly hatched butterfly die. During the struggle to emerge from the cocoon, the caterpillar will struggle, then stop, struggle some more, and stop again, until enough fluid from its head is forced into its wings in order for it to fly. The painful transformation is necessary to allow others to grow; it is hard to watch others experience it firsthand, but we must allow the metamorphosis to occur. Now, this doesn't mean we shouldn't help those around us that are hurting or try to ease their pain in some way. But we shouldn't attempt to completely remove or circumvent their circumstances, so they will grow and mature. Neither should we make fun of others' pain or consider ourselves more important, since we aren't struggling at this particular time. We never know when we could be next; the safety and security that we feel in our job, relationship, etc. is only an illusion. That rug could be pulled out from under any one of us at any moment.

He that is discontented in one place will seldom be content in another.

Aesop

Beware discontentment and the "Rags-to-Riches" myth. We all have a tendency to desire the opposite of what we have; the idea that the opposite will make us happy is a mirage at best and a destructive force in our lives at worst. Rather than being thankful for what we do have, we choose to focus on what we don't have. If we succumb to the temptation of discontentment, we are more vulnerable to affairs, fraud, more discontentment, etc., than we would ever be under normal circumstances. This is a time where logic is thrown out in favor of emotion, and damaging, life-altering decisions are made accordingly.

We tend to gloss over the depth, severity, and length of adversity that gave birth to great success. We have all read stories about larger-than-life figures who overcame incredible odds to achieve great things in politics, business, education, etc. We must realize that the story we are sold makes for an inspiring read, but it is usually light on the full details of the "rags" phase of the rags-to-riches story. Let's resolve to keep that in perspective the next time we read one of those stories. We should be inspired that we can all achieve success in some area of life. If someone is hugely successful, know that it most likely took years or decades to build and prepare to achieve that. And remember that accomplishment might come in an unexpected area of life (like your family), and triumph is not always about money or other tangible things.

Don't forget where you came from. The nameplate I keep on my desk is one from several jobs ago, when I was a used car salesman. Don't laugh–we aren't all dirty, rotten scoundrels. I wasn't perfect, but I tried to be an honest salesman. Believe it or not; there are just as many lying customers as there are lying salespeople. I keep that particular nameplate on my desk no matter what position I currently have, to remind me of those times. I'm not remembering those days with longing; instead, I remember how hard things were and how much I learned about life and myself in that pressure-cooker environment. I don't want to forget my humble beginnings. Selling used cars, applying pest control, shipping and receiving, talking to upset customers, mowing lawns, and every job I've had since, has prepared me in some way for my current job, and the job I have now is preparing me for some other job in the future. Don't despise the day of small beginnings.

24

A Time for Emotion and a Time for Stoicism

Much as the wisdom of Solomon admonishes us that "there is a season, a time for every activity under heaven,"[13] there is a time to display emotion (sorrow, anger, etc.) and a time for a lack of emotional display. At times, we as leaders must remain in control of our emotions in the heat of the moment when others around us are losing their cool. Otherwise, they will not look to us to lead them if we are cowering in the foxhole with them. This doesn't mean we should ignore our emotions; we just don't have the luxury as leaders to lose our composure by showing our personal disappointment at a public company meeting. We must choose the right venue to share our deepest fears and failures. At the same time, we need to allow others to see us cry once in a while at an appropriate time and venue, so that we aren't perceived as emotionless as Data from Star Trek.

At the appropriate time, it is vital to reveal the battle scars that we've incurred along the way so that others can relate to us. They learn that we all struggle and have wounds; leaders are not some superhuman race that never bleeds. All of us have issues and pains, and it helps others to understand us better if we let down our emotional wall to disclose our pains, struggles, and failures. They need to see this, since it will encourage them to have hope in their ostensibly challenging situation. It also humanizes leaders and abolishes the idea that leaders are above problems the underlings have to deal with. We all put our pants on one leg at a time.

We shouldn't allow people to get under our skin. The only way people can gain control over your emotions is to allow them to. It is up to us to determine how we behave; our emotions and the emotions of others don't control us unless we let them. I learned this from a friend of mine, Rob, who learned it the hard way. He used to let his boss dictate his mood and emotions, and it made him miserable. Rob would remind me not to let others get under my skin, and I am grateful for those constant reminders during the two years he and I worked together. I realize this is hard for all of us; quite frankly, this is still hard for me to do. But we owe it to those closest to us not to allow ourselves to get caught up in this, since doing so will only lead to us venting to those closest to us and causing them to carry our stress.

Leaders use their heart as well as their head. After they have looked at the facts with their head, they let their heart take a look too.

Robert K. Greenleaf

Men sometimes speak as if humility and meekness would rob us of what is noble and bold and manlike. O that all would believe that this is the nobility of the kingdom of heaven, that this is the royal spirit that the King of heaven displayed, that this is Godlike, to humble oneself, to become the servant of all!

Andrew Murray

Meekness initially defers to others and is the openness to being corrected and directed; leaders that are meek are sensitive, patient, and long-suffering. Don't mock meekness in leaders, because it ain't weakness. Sensitive people can develop a tough skin while maintaining a soft heart. You will find strength and depth of character in sensitive people who have learned how not to dissolve into a puddle at the first sign of resistance. These people are rare, since most sensitive people tend to get so beat up by our uncaring world around them and either become cold and calloused or turn to mush at any hardship. Those who keep their sensitivity intact are compassionate, caring, warm, and thoughtful, but not necessarily weak in spirit. Many are much stronger in their convictions and strength of character as a result. Lack of respect for meek, sensitive people reveals a shallow and foolish spirit.

25

Wrap-up

Adversity must be weathered if we are to withstand the burden of authority and power that comes with leadership; without struggle, we have a tendency to crumble under the stress and pressure. Authentic leadership is following through on our promises and focusing more on substance than style. We don't seek celebrity but are more often than not uncomfortable and reluctant to be in the spotlight.

PART 4

Specific Management Situations: Getting Results

While I have talked mostly in general terms about how to lead, this final section will be more specific about common small-business situations. Topics to be discussed are managing up and across organizations, capitalism, economics, shareholder value, marketing, and writing skills. You may wonder what any of these have to do with leadership, but each of them are areas where many of today's small-business leaders are not leading well. Review or reexamine these topics and challenge your preconceived notions about them.

26

Management Ain't a Dirty Word

Leaders create plans and set them in motion. They are people of thought and action, both dreamers and doers. They are self-starters.

Robert K. Greenleaf

To idealize "leadership" and demean "management," as is currently in vogue in business literature, makes being the boss harder, since you need both leadership and management skills to be a successful leader. Management and leadership have sadly been separately defined and disassociated, but the best leaders exhibit both, and perhaps we should only have one term that encompasses both distinctions. Consider the legendary Peter Drucker: He is considered the father of modern *management* theory and philosophy, but you will not find a better writer on *leadership* principles anywhere. The elevation of "leadership" over "management" is another example of how our culture routinely latches onto new buzzwords.

Leadership and management are not separate disciplines as some would have you believe. At the same time, they are not synonyms; there is a real distinction between the vision-oriented leadership role of a CEO (Chief Executive

Officer) and the management-oriented role of a COO (Chief Operating Officer). But saying they are separate disciplines misses the important fact that to be successful at a high level, we need both. They are interdependent disciplines, and the best managers/leaders can both inspire people (leadership) and hold them accountable for work that needs to be done (management). Some leadership authors today say we need more leaders and fewer managers; I say we need people who are skilled at both and know how to seamlessly switch between their manager and leader hats. Most people in a leadership position will find that they are stronger in one area than the other. But with the business environment changing so rapidly, we cannot afford to simply excuse ourselves from half of our work because it isn't our strength. We must rise to the challenge and learn how to get better in our area of weakness. The best leaders can look up and outside the organization (vision) as a CEO would and nearly simultaneously look down and in (management of operations) as a COO would. Those who can juggle both roles well will be more successful in business and life.

Think of and refer to your organization's members as a team, not a family. A family cannot fire its members, but a team can get rid of underperformers if it is in the best interest of the whole.[14] This will change your outlook from one of paternalism to one that seeks what is best for the team. You might be surprised at how poorly many organizations do with this. They either can't let anyone go or hold on to people whom the organization has outgrown. This creates inefficiencies, since the world is always changing rapidly. Another rather simple goal is to use "we" instead of "I" in your daily conversation. When I realized how often I use "I" in my speech, I was somewhat embarrassed that I was so self-centered. When we replace it with "we", we speak loud and clear to our team that we are in this together. We win together; we lose together. Sharing in the success and failure strengthens the team dynamic. Intentionally using the word "we" instead of "I" won't shift the team dynamic in and of itself; it is symbolic and is complimentary to actions the leader is taking to build the team.

Don't forget to manage your boss. Either we brag and take credit for projects our team members had more to do with than us, or we never allow our boss to see our impact by keeping silent or allowing others to take credit from us. How about balancing both of those by keeping the boss in the loop on your work? Let them see your achievements without bragging. It is our responsibility to "manage up" as well as down, meaning we need to manage our boss's expectations by regularly asking for feedback. While bosses should give us that customary advice without our prodding, it is up to us to draw it out of them. If we wait for them to approach us, at best we may never get the feedback we need to grow professionally, thus hindering our career prospects. At worst, we might get fired or laid off due to being oblivious to our poor performance.

We need to be aware of the different, figurative hats we wear in managing relationships with others, especially when we wear several hats within the same organization. It is important to take these "hats" off and on as appropriate and verbalize to others what hat you are wearing. For instance, I am both a parent and a board member at my children's private school. When I go in for parent-teacher conferences, I must remind the teacher which hat I am wearing, so the teacher doesn't assume I am speaking with the authority of a board member when I am actually speaking as a dad. I once heard of a story where a father made the choice to fire his son. The father called his son into his office, and said, "I am going to have to fire you for not fulfilling the expectations of your job. Now I am taking off my manager 'hat' and putting on my dad 'hat'." As he went over and placed his arm around his son, he said, "I am very sorry you lost your job today." As hard as that is, we have to distinguish between the conflicting roles we hold and clearly communicate from which role we are speaking.

Anything with more than two heads is a freak, not a management team.

Management by consensus/committee is a recipe for disaster. While I am in favor of having a deep leadership bench/management team, there should be only one final play caller (to use a football metaphor). I am amazed at how certain companies think they can have co-CEOs, make decisions by committee/consensus, or otherwise have more than one final decision maker. Maybe they split up what types of decisions get made by whom, but in a company with two leaders, who is watching out for the overall best interest of the company? I am sure that there are exceptions to this rule, but generally speaking, having more than one person ultimately in charge is a disaster waiting to happen. Don't get me wrong, soliciting many perspectives in search of the best decision/solution is a decidedly positive thing, but it is imperative to choose only one leader to make the final call.

Most boards of directors are disorganized, dysfunctional, and/or don't know what they are doing because they have poor leadership. Most don't follow *Robert's Rules of Order*, thinking it is irrelevant, unneeded, or too rigid. Most don't hold board members accountable, don't have a strong recruitment and selection process, and become ineffective at best in their oversight of management. People join boards for the wrong reasons: to be part of a social club or to rubber-stamp management's decisions. And the primary blame for all of these shortcomings lies at the feet of the chairman of the board. Now, we don't need wildly intrusive boards that overstep their bounds and get into the day-to-day management of the company. But we must have healthy board stewardship so that managers don't have too long of an accountability leash. We need directors to work with top management to set the strategy of the company and then allow the managers to execute on this plan, not second-guessing or meddling in company affairs. If we have weaker leaders as managers, then the board is forced to step up and take a bit more of an active role in oversight of the organization. By the same token, if we have stronger leadership in management, the board should allow the managers a bit freer rein without completely shirking their oversight responsibility. I must thank Terry Kohler for being a solid example of a balanced approach as chairman of a company I used to manage; Terry took a more "hands off" approach by allowing management to make decisions rather than allowing the board to micromanage, but would step in when appropriate to hold management accountable for its actions.

Don't automatically equate success with solid leadership/management. "Correlation doesn't mean causality" was a mantra I heard in my graduate work at The Spears School of Business at Oklahoma State University. It is this rule that I have applied to what appears to be success on the surface. I have been fortunate to be a part of a number of businesses that appeared successful on the outside. But in several of those cases, there were significant problems with talent, operations, and/or cash-flow management. I recommend we take the time to ask the right questions to ferret out whether this business is just lucky, or whether they are lucky *and* have talented management. Many owners/entrepreneurs are not equipped with the skills to lead and manage the multifaceted needs of an organization over the long term. They are successful for a time by the sheer force of their will, pushing their organizations to have a certain level of success. Most companies would benefit highly from hiring an outside business professional to run things or a consultant to give them the advice they need to be even more successful. But if the leaders never learn how to be better leaders and work on the business (or hire someone who can lead and manage), the company will plateau at best and tank at worst.

27

Capitalism and Economics

Capitalism always squeezes out inefficiencies and costs, so our choice is to squeeze (ourselves) or be squeezed. Whether we like it or not, and whether we elect to implement it or it is forced on us by the marketplace, capitalism seeks to lower cost wherever and whenever it can. Competition has a built-in continual improvement mechanism, but some businesses act like it doesn't exist. We can choose to ignore this law of capitalism and get pummeled by our competitors who are focused on becoming more efficient, or we can recognize it and seek to become experts in continuous improvement techniques. Some techniques to investigate are LEAN, Value-Stream Mapping, Six Sigma, and 5S.

Relentless pursuit of incremental growth and efficiency should be our focus. Lexus's slogan used to be "The Relentless Pursuit of Perfection," which embodies the ethos most companies need if they want long-term, multigenerational, enduring success. We must choose to pursue continuous improvement—especially when things are going well. Competition always gravitates toward squeezing out costs and inefficiencies. If you get fat, dumb, and happy, you may last for a while, but eventually some competitor will find a cheaper, more efficient, better way to serve your customers at higher quality and lower cost. Then you slide towards irrelevance and eventual capitulation and don't usually realize why. We need to resist the urge to rest on our laurels. We should use every opportunity to continually and relentlessly better our business position rather than think we have vanquished our opposition.

Stash cash during the boom, and spend like you stole it during the bust. A religious, almost fanatical, attention to cash flow during positive and negative times is a hallmark of well-run companies, and lack thereof is a harbinger of failed ones. So let's save cash when business is booming and spend it more generously during recessionary times. There will be lots of opportunities to invest in profitable projects and marketing expenses in order to gain market share while other companies are retreating. Many companies operate in just the opposite manner, pulling back spending on marketing, advertising, and R&D in recessionary times. We have the opportunity to gain market share from our competitors if we zig when they zag. But the only way to do that is to prepare by saving during the best of times.

Organizations who think they are maintaining/holding ground are mistaken. You are either growing or dying.

Jim Collins

Companies decline slowly. Once an organization has generated a decent level of success and momentum over several years, it can take longer to decline than most might think. Even if there are signs of team dysfunction, poor cash-flow management, or high employee turnover or dissatisfaction, an organization can go on for quite a while by cutting expenses until there isn't enough revenue to continue. I have witnessed firsthand companies that were in various stages of decline, and I and others marveled at how long they kept going while their revenue and market influence was waning, even those I thought were already knocking on death's door. Most companies with a decent amount of cash from previous boom years can "ride the company down" by cutting expenses every year and/or subsidizing from a war chest of cash elsewhere, giving the illusion that everything is okay. Other symptoms of decay are stubbornly high levels of employee turnover, continuous loss of key customers, delayed payroll, vital equipment sales, shortened credit terms, bills being paid much later than normal, etc. Companies can keep running with these symptoms for a long time, but make no mistake, the company is in decline internally even if it is not visible to outsiders. Don't underestimate how long a poorly run company can last before they capitulate to bankruptcy or shutdown. Eventually, a company can no longer cut anymore and must sell (an unlikely prospect since there usually isn't much to sell at this point) or file bankruptcy. Let's not allow our organizations to get to this point; let's take the proactive steps to keep our companies healthy. Check out the book *How the Mighty Fall: And Why Some Never Give In* for more insight on how some companies have reversed decline.

I have become fascinated over the last couple of years with the interconnectivity of global economies and the implications for governments, businesses, and individuals, since it has so much impact on companies small and large.[15] And with the increasing complexity of various moving economic parts, we as leaders in business must pay more attention to economic principles. In the past, our economy in America was relatively simple and isolated, and we didn't need to pay attention to what happened outside our borders to run our business. In the coming years, companies that fail to monitor world macroeconomics will be at a disadvantage in analyzing and planning for how their industry will be affected by the changing environment. Those that fail to pay attention will risk losing customers or even go out of business completely.

While I am certain there are many other laws of economic physics, I have chosen to focus on three of them that are directly applicable to business leadership.

1. What goes up (overinflated markets/bubbles) must come down.
2. Overindebtedness eventually leads to default in some form (personal, government, or corporate).
3. There are always unintended economic consequences to economic actions.

The first law is illustrated by reviewing the U.S. mortgage crisis/housing bubble; during the bubble inflation stage, more and more people chant, "This time is different." They irrationally propose that the prosperity mania will continue forever (i.e., house prices will never fall), and eventually the house of cards falls and the market resets. If we can spot economic bubbles forming, we may be able to prepare our businesses and weather the storm better than our competitors, which benefits team members, customers, and shareholders alike.

The second law states that once a person, corporation, or government reaches their "credit limit," markets revolt and refuse to continue lending on such generous terms. Even the vaunted U.S. federal government has a credit limit; the problem is we just don't know when the bond markets will require a substantially higher risk premium in the form of higher interest payments. Both of these laws are incredibly important to business leaders, since both federal and state governments are overleveraged and hemorrhaging cash in the form of reduced tax receipts across nearly all categories of tax revenues.

The third law can be quite dangerous, especially when those implementing the action haven't adequately or thoughtfully considered the ramifications economic consequences. While we cannot foresee all possible scenarios, leaders, especially in politics, must more seriously consider the unintended consequences to actions that are to be implemented.

Just as the rich rule the poor, so the borrower is servant to the lender.

Proverbs 22:7, NLT

In my graduate school finance courses, the virtues of leverage were extolled. Interest payments, not dividends, are tax deductible; this encouraged companies over the last several decades to lever up with more debt and less equity. What the U.S. government failed to realize is that we are encouraging businesses to engage in riskier and riskier behavior in order to minimize taxes. While I am not completely opposed to debt (whether corporate or personal), we must be much more careful now than we were in the past. With high levels of debt, companies are much less able to service their debt if they lose a significant amount of revenue. It's prudent to keep debt to a minimum. We can't always count on consistent revenue, even if we are delivering good quality, prices, and customer service. Sometimes we lose accounts due to no fault of our own when the economy tightens up. The developed world is in for a bumpy, slow-growth, protracted recessionary environment over the next several years. These are all reasons to be a bit more careful when considering more leverage.

On top of the growth of corporate leverage, individuals have added mountains of debt over the last couple of decades. The growth in our global economy over the last couple of decades is mainly a direct result of American consumption fueled by leverage. This explains the world-wide economic difficulties following the American housing bubble. Americans have been the largest group of consumers in the world, and with our economy suffering, the countries who have been producing our consumer goods can't export as much. So that depresses their economies, and the cycle continues. We need a return to producing and exporting goods from the U.S. This will begin to reverse the trade deficit that fuels our government's addiction to borrowing from China and other exporters of goods to America. Rather than spending all of our money consuming goods, U.S. citizens ought to start saving a higher percentage of our income. I know this will depress GDP further in the short term, but we need to change our financial behavior and addiction to personal debt as part of the solution to our long-term government debt crisis. But we will not encourage saving with the Fed holding interest rates artificially low, since savers are forced to invest in riskier assets in search of a higher return, which can cause many of them to lose their savings when these riskier assets go bust.

I am as economical as the next guy, but insurance is one of those areas we shouldn't scrimp on. Leaders focus on the long-term advantage of having adequate insurance coverage for their organization or family. The marginal cost of over-insuring is minimal compared to the potential cost of a catastrophe. Yet every day, people try to buy the cheapest life, disability, auto, home, renters, umbrella, or other form of insurance, just to save a few bucks each year. Most don't buy term life or disability insurance. While I strongly urge you to have term life insurance, it's even more important to have disability on major income earners in your family. You are nearly four times more likely to be disabled than to die.

In fact, the vast majority of wealthy people don't "self-insure" as us middle class people assume they do; self-insuring consists of NOT buying any insurance, instead choosing to cover catastrophic losses with one's own cash. Most wealthy people still carry high levels of insurance because they are hedging against the same level of risk the rest of us MUST avoid. So stop trying to save a few bucks; if and when you have a catastrophic loss on something of value, you will be glad you didn't under-insure. I've even heard of a company that was looking to lower their group health insurance premiums and was told they should drastically increase their plan deductible from $1,000 to $5,000. This would significantly lower their premiums; then they told team members that they would cover any difference in deductible that a team member incurred. This is another example of short-term gain and long-term pain; it completely undermines the entire philosophy behind insurance (shifting risk to a third party), since the company is now on the hook for the deductible difference of $4,000 per employee that triggers that higher deductible claim. The company is increasing its risk disproportionally to the comparatively minimal amount of premium dollar savings. Pay the higher premiums to hedge against potential, catastrophic, upside risk. Even though an event like this is highly unlikely, it is wiser to pay the slightly higher premium. Always carry slightly more insurance than you need. I have term life policies on myself and my wife, a disability policy on myself, auto insurance, renter's policy, and an umbrella policy to cover additional accidental liability. I just never know when I will need to use any of them. And if I never use them, I haven't wasted all of those premium dollars. I exchanged monies to insure against potential losses.

28

Stop Destroying Shareholder Value

Nearly two-thirds of companies now destroy value (earned shareholder returns [dividends + stock price appreciation] below inflation), according to a recent Bain & Company study. The study also uncovered the statistic that only 9% of companies achieve even a modest level of sustained and profitable growth. This is insane; what are we paying top management to do all day? Chris Zook and James Allen point to four key rules that companies should follow to increase shareholder value.

1. Build intolerance for excess complexity.
2. Compete for the long term.
3. Focus on your greatest strengths.
4. Make strategy a search for a repeatable model that can replicate and adapt your greatest successes again and again.

Please heed this warning and stop destroying your company's value; in many small-business cases, the owner/entrepreneur and/or management is violating all four rules unknowingly. They either don't know what they don't know or aren't paying attention to the bigger picture. Because of technology, never in the history of the world has it been easier to learn what you don't know or find someone who does know and can help bring strong management skills to your organization. There are no excuses not to find others to fill in our areas of weakness.

Some people aren't used to an environment where excellence is expected.

Steve Jobs

Aim for excellence. So much in our world is done sloppily and carelessly, and we are all capable of doing better than that. What if we all worked just a little bit harder to bring excellence into every area of our lives? What if we strove for excellence in our schools, homes, businesses, and (God forbid) government? But shooting for excellence is hard. It requires extra effort and is often not fun in the short term. It is more work, but in the long run, the fruit of our additional labor is totally worth it. And striving for excellence means we must choose what to be involved in and, more importantly, what activities to pass up. We must not overcommit to too many projects; then we can focus on the few projects and dedicate our time to excellence in those areas. In today's culture, we tend to prefer convenience over excellence. We are impatient and want to get results with minimal effort, certainly with no amount of sacrifice. Choose excellence over convenience; we will all reap huge dividends if we choose wisely.

Look for arbitrage and be opportunistic. Investopedia's definition of arbitrage is "the simultaneous purchase and sale of an asset in order to profit from a difference in the price. It is a trade that profits by exploiting price differences of identical or similar financial instruments, on different markets or in different forms."[16] While some look down on opportunism in business generally and arbitrage specifically, it is simply shrewd of leaders to look for arbitrage prospects whether in a boom or bust cycle. These breaks don't come around very often, and we shouldn't shy away from uncovering every opportunity we can, even if it is an unrelated industry.

The show doesn't go on because it's ready. The show goes on because it's 11:30.

Lorne Michaels

Launch and ship when "good enough." Too often we wait too long to unveil our product or service. It is our duty to launch our product or service when it's "good enough" and let the market vet its success or failure. Those of us who are perfectionists are typically the worst at this; we want to get it perfect before moving forward. But the key here is that until the product or service is being sold, the idea is not generating any sales. Sales pay the bills and generate profits and cash flow. The sooner it is "good enough" and launched, the closer we all are to getting paid—owners, managers, team members, customers, etc. Too many entrepreneurs and businesses hold on to their ideas for far too long before bringing them to market. While there are many reasons for this, most notably fear and procrastination. We must reject the excuses and accept the challenge Seth Godin gave us to "ship stuff today." Don't wait for tomorrow; it never comes. And the world needs those new ideas to be shared because they can make others' lives richer, healthier, and wiser. And the worst that can happen is that your product or service doesn't sell and you learn more about yourself in the process in order to retool the product or service or expose new avenues of life that you never would've experienced otherwise. So what are you waiting for?

Rely on data to drive decisions. It's dangerous for leaders to make decisions predominantly based on recollection and anecdotes, since we can lead our organizations down the completely wrong path. Let's not be overconfident in our ability to lead based on limited information. Now, we don't want analysis paralysis, waiting indefinitely for perfect information, but let's get info that is as accurate as possible and then make a decision. There is no such thing as perfect information; even the largest and most prepared companies don't have perfect information. All business decisions have an inherent uncertainty present, some more or less than others. Thinking that if our organizations just get larger, smarter, etc., we will escape the dangers of uncertainty is plain naïve. Sometimes we do need to trust our gut or anecdotes to make decisions; but let's reach for the data first and make "gut feel" the exception after we have applied the rule.

There is no presumption of innocence when it comes to ideas. All ideas are bad until proven otherwise. Too often we become enamored of an idea that popped up in some meeting. We run off and implement it with little thought, research, or understanding. I am not saying that we should be too skeptical of new ideas either; we must balance being skeptical enough with not being too cynical. New ideas should be evaluated against our personal or corporate core values and goals, financial considerations, time constraints, as well as other important, meaningful standards. Let's be careful we don't allow our families or organizations to be constantly lurching from one new idea to the next without vetting and giving it adequate time to take hold.

Look for a complex explanation, not a simplistic one. Look for multiple causes and explanations for problems. Rarely is it just one solitary thing, but it's human nature to oversimplify in search of one root cause in order to assign it blame. Doing so gives the false sense that if we just fix this one thing, we will perform better. Or if it is something outside our control, we have a tendency to throw our hands up in the air and think there is nothing to do to address the problem. There are always levers we can pull to try to turn things around. Usually this means being aware of what we truly cannot control and choosing to focus on what we can control.

Simply because things will likely change does not give us an excuse not to make plans.

The worst thing we can do as leaders is to lurch from tactic to tactic like the fox in Jim Collins's book *Good to Great*. If you haven't read it, you should. Here is an excerpt from Jim Collins explaining the fox and the hedgehog.

> Picture two animals: a fox and a hedgehog. Which are you? An ancient Greek parable distinguishes between foxes, which know many small things, and hedgehogs, which know one big thing. All Level 5 leaders, it turns out, are hedgehogs. They know how to simplify a complex world into a single, organizing idea—the kind of basic principle that unifies, organizes, and guides all decisions. That's not to say hedgehogs are simplistic. Like great thinkers, who take complexities and boil them down into simple, yet profound, ideas (Adam Smith and the invisible hand, Darwin and evolution), leaders of good-to-great companies develop a Hedgehog Concept that is simple but that reflects penetrating insight and deep understanding.

It is much better to define the strategy for your organization, family, etc., and then determine what tactics to utilize in the pursuit of that overarching strategy. Unfortunately, most organizations, especially smaller ones, lurch from one "great" idea to the next "great" idea rather than sticking to their core, niche businesses and being the best at that. For more information on the topic of strategy, check out Steve VanRemortel's book *Stop Selling Vanilla Ice Cream*. So please either hire others to help you plan and execute a strategy or sell your company to someone who will.

In the name of all that is holy, if you hire consultants, please take their advice and use it. I am so sick of hearing this story: A company spends tens, if not hundreds, of thousands of dollars on consultants, who create a strategy and tactics for the business to follow. The consultants package their advice into a hefty 100-page three-ring binder, which the company leaders almost immediately put on a shelf somewhere. They either implement none of it or so very little of it as to not impact the organization in any meaningful way. This is a result of business owners or managers realizing they need to do something different (engaging the consultant) but not really wanting to change (little implementation). If you aren't ready to change and implement most of what a consultant is going to suggest, then don't waste your money or the consultant's time in the first place. Save the money—you will need it to keep your company on life support. If your company is dying, it's time to get over your own arrogance and fear to change and listen to some good advice.

Don't step over dollars to save dimes. Usually, companies' top expense is wages and salaries, so those naturally will be at the top of the list in terms of consideration for budget cuts. If you are forced to make budgetary cuts, I don't recommend making an across-the-board percentage cut in pay or hours, since it inflicts pain on both the high performers and weaker team members alike. This sends a message to our top performers that performance isn't that important. Rather, I recommend cutting positions and reallocating job duties with the remaining staff. Focus on those who are your lowest performers and cut those positions; that will send a clear message to your team that top job performance is highly valued and poor performance will not be accepted. Other top expenses must be considered in addition to salaries and wages, but we must be careful neither to cut too deeply nor too shallowly. It is a delicate balance, and one should consider how each cut will ultimately affect all stakeholders (customers, team members, and shareholders). I advise erring slightly on the side of cutting more than you have to, so it is less likely that you will need another round of cuts in a few weeks or months.

You would be amazed at how few people calculate the money value of their time and will spend too much time trying to get a vendor to reduce their cell phone bill by $5. We should be somewhat frugal with our money as good stewards should, but if the amount of money we're trying to recoup is more than the amount of time to complete the task multiplied by our hourly rate, then we should not waste our precious time resources on that activity. Intangible factors, such as our time, are rarely factored into the equation. This consideration goes for team members who work for us as well. If we are paying an assistant $10 an hour to save $20 on something by driving around town for 2 hours, we should recognize that this is highly illogical, miserly, and is only a break-even proposition. We must ask ourselves about other intangible costs as well, like how much stress will this add to our lives just to save a couple of bucks. We should allow ourselves to spend more money to get more of that intangible.

> I have often advised managers that a 20-to-one salary ratio [of their salary to the median worker's salary] is the limit beyond which they cannot go if they don't want resentment and falling morale to hit their companies.

Peter Drucker

Have you ever found yourself jealous or envious (they are different emotions) of someone in senior management? It is quite hard not to desire the perks, power, influence, and money that those at the top have. And while jealousy and envy are morally wrong, as leaders in senior management, it is our duty not to allow executive compensation, perks, etc., to get out of hand. As Mr. Drucker so aptly stated, we should keep total executive pay to no more than a 20-to-one salary ratio (executive to average team member) to avoid the perception of managerial overcompensation. The key word is perception, and each company is different. While a 20-to-one ratio may work for one company, it may not for another organization that needs a 10-to-one ratio. We should try to put ourselves in our average team member's shoes and ask ourselves if the pay spread is truly fair.

> Leaders consider others to be their partners in the work and see to it that they share in the rewards.

Robert K. Greenleaf

I want to caution others to ease up on performance-based pay; I lean more towards paying team members generous base pay and supplementing them minimally on performance. This doesn't mean we shouldn't monitor team member performance; far from it. If they are performing well, then increase their base pay. Don't tempt them, since too much incentive pay tends to focus people's attention on gaming the system to gain as much bonus pay as possible. At a job I had early on in my career, every other month certain sales people would game the system by forcing new sales (service contracts) through that were either not signed by the customer yet or were bogus sales contracts in order to maximize their bonuses. On the "off" months, they would have many of these contracts cancel for obvious reasons and have little to no bonus on those months. But the "on" months were highly lucrative for them, since their higher commission percentage with higher sales volumes more than made up for the "off" months. Besides being an issue of fraud, these sales people harmed the company's reputation. Sadly, these situations focus some people on what personally benefits them at the expense of the customer or company. So be careful when putting together performance-based pay plans. If performance-based pay is important to you, it is even more important to hire highly morally focused team members who will do the right thing for the customer and organization regardless of pay.

Don't be small because you can't figure out how to get big. Consider being small because it might be better.

Seth Godin

Smaller and slower is smarter. Hint: bigger and faster is not. Economies of scale aren't always beneficial; often times smaller and nimbler is better. It is tough for entrepreneurs and small organizations with high aspirations to embrace being small. They want to change the world,

163

or at least unseat the industry leader. The ironic thing is that in choosing to be small and focused on our own business (as opposed to worrying and obsessing about the competition), we end up achieving success on our own terms by serving our customers in a unique way. And we don't allow ourselves to be distracted by adopting the tactics of other companies, since we know the right ones for our own customers. Ignore your competitors' tactics, serve your customers with excellence, and be satisfied with serving a smaller niche. You can do this much better than larger competitors can. Choose to be small and remarkable (delighting customers along the way) rather than large and boring.

Going public through an IPO ain't all it's cracked up to be. The number of publicly listed companies on U.S. exchanges has fallen from 8,823 in 1997, at the height of the dot-com boom, to under 5,000 at the end of 2011, according to the World Federation of Exchanges. More companies held IPOs (initial public offerings) between 1996 and 1997 than in the entire decade between 2001 and 2011. Many companies have learned the hard way that an IPO shouldn't always be the goal; just ask Univision, Aramark, Yankee Candle, Jacuzzi Brands, HCA, Harrah's, or Cablevision, who have all gone private in recent years. In fact, keeping a company private or taking one private has many advantages, not the least of which is the ability of the management team to manage for the long term instead of the short term. Public companies are almost always focused on meeting the next quarter's financial numbers and analysts' expectations, plus the added regulation of Sarbanes-Oxley. The major downside for investors of private companies is the lack of liquidity. But if cash is being handled properly in a private organization, investors should be able to receive either dividends or share buybacks on a regular basis to accommodate their compensation requirements.

Have you ever heard the statement, "We can't keep up with the growth in sales, but that's a good problem to have." Poppycock, I say; there is a fallacy in that statement. Sustained, controlled growth is healthier and less disruptive than explosive growth. It's counterintuitive, but growing a business slower will almost always help you achieve your goals faster. That's right; slower is faster. Business history is littered with companies that grew too quickly and ran into problems. Choose to pull back on the reins and grow incrementally and in a controlled, planned way rather than allowing ego to drive the organization towards fast growth. Explosive growth is nearly always destructive to the culture, cash flow, and overall feel of the company, and for this reason, explosive growth should be avoided in almost all circumstances. Another downside to explosive growth is that we assume we can maintain high growth rates year after year. That gets harder and harder to do, disappointing team members and leading ultimately to disillusionment with management's ability to grow the company. Sonic Drive-In is one company that has chosen to control and limit their growth to a certain number of stores per year. We need more companies like Sonic Drive-In that understand the wisdom of incremental and sustained growth over decades. We don't need any more companies that are a "flash in the pan"; rather, we need organizations that are slow-burning candles. The latter will light the way for others to follow.

29

Marketing and Mad Writing
Skills Wanted

Social Media sites like Twitter, Facebook, Linkedin and YouTube are changing the way the world does business. I think this is in response to our desire to connect with others. Relationship Marketing is all about connecting with people first as human beings and then as customers later. For a real business relationship to work, both parties must receive value. If only one or neither does, that relationship won't continue for long.

Terry Brock

Relational, not transactional business is the goal. Organizations that focus on developing relationships with their customers and serving the customer both before and after the sale will win in the long term. Those focused solely on making the sale today might make more sales in the short term. But in the long term, they will continually have to find more transactions. Meanwhile, the relationship-focused organization can rely on referral after referral. Show the customer you have their best interest at heart regardless of whether you ever earn their business, and you will almost never have to search for another transaction sale. People desire relationship, even in business.

However, we must never confuse this with putting the relationship ahead of business interests. Business must be first and relationship second. Many allow their personal friendships to cloud their judgment in business. This may happen in hiring someone you know who is not the right fit for a particular position, or it may take the form of choosing to do business with a vendor exclusively on the basis of friendship. At best, the former leads to frustration by other team members, and at worst, it leads to your top performers leaving your company. The latter will blind you to a vendor overcharging and might even dupe you into accepting lower quality standards or customer service. These vendors aren't true friends; otherwise, the natural friendship would flow out of a respect for delivering quality performance. The work should be done early or on time, priced competitively, and customer-serviced with excellence. If friendship blossoms as a result, then that is all the better. Remember, business is first; relationship is second.

Don't Sell the Steak – Sell the Sizzle!

Elmer Wheeler

Chip Heath and Dan Heath encourage us to tell concrete stories to illustrate what we are trying to communicate or teach others. They explain that the more we learn and become experts in our field, the more we tend to speak in technical jargon and abstractions that only a few understand instead of concrete facts that most comprehend easily. We have a habit of unknowingly complicating our explanation of things because we have expert knowledge.

While we shouldn't stop learning and growing our knowledge, we should be aware of our natural tendency to speak abstractly. The simplest way to speak more concretely is to use stories to explain things. Stories are more memorable and stickier, so if you want others to remember what you told them, find stories to illustrate things.

Seth Godin encourages us to tell stories about how our products or services will make people feel. For example, I used to work for a company that sold skin care products. We weren't selling a pill to clear acne; we were selling relief from the emotional and physical pain (embarrassment, social stigma, etc.) of acne. At another organization, we sold DVDs, books, and seminar tickets for marriage enrichment, but we weren't really selling DVDs and books. We were selling marriage medicine that was wrapped in laughter, so the bitter-tasting pill would go down more easily. And we were also selling emotional relief from marital discord.

Lagniappe is a word with Spanish and French origins that means giving something extra for good measure, like the thirteenth roll in a baker's dozen. This is one of the ways that we can be memorable. When my family and I visited Blue Harbor Resort[17] in Sheboygan, WI, the housekeeping staff not only cleaned our room each day, they placed our three children's teddy bears with care at strategic places in the room, as if they were live Smith family members. One was sitting on the bed, another on the table, and the last one was lounging on the couch. Those housekeepers didn't HAVE to do that, but they did. And we will remember that for a long time, which makes us more likely to stay there again and refer others to stay there too.

A friend of mine was on a business trip, flying Southwest Airlines, and had his initial flight delayed so long that he was going to miss his connecting flight. Yet when he arrived at his connecting gate after running through multiple terminals, he was stunned to find they were holding the plane solely for him. He was floored and to this day tells others about that story. Talk about powerful and free marketing! We all need to practice giving something unanticipated to our customers, team members, families, and friends. Maybe it is an unexpected kind word for a job well done or an extra case of product for a loyal customer or staying late to help a customer in need when we didn't have to. The emotion of that moment will stick in the other's memory, which will cause them to remember that moment repeatedly in the future. It is amazing how something so simple can last as a memory for decades. Think of it this way; why should people remember us? Are our actions worth remembering and remarking about? If not, endeavor to create habits that are memory worthy.

The business model "build it and they will come" used to work when there was scarcity of information, but in our information-rich, digital age, products or services are either becoming remarkable or becoming irrelevant. In today's internet world, it is just that simple, as much as we might wish for the "olden days" to return. We can no longer rely on the tried and true method of spending a ton of money on a product, service, ad space, etc. and expecting people to show up to purchase what we are selling. However, "build something remarkable, and they will come" is very much alive. Focus on creating something of significant value that is remarkable, and the world just might beat a path to your door if you are persistent. It is certainly no guarantee, but it beats the heck out of spending tons of money to find out that no one wants to buy what you are selling. Large facilities, ad campaigns, signage, etc., are being replaced by more nimble competitors doing more with less. We must be wiser, faster and have a better service and/or product in order to succeed these days, and even that doesn't assure victory.

There is no business without a customer.

Peter Drucker

Don't fool yourself that a successful business plan opens or closes with the line, "If we just capture 1% of the market, we will make tons of money." Do your market research and come up with a credible plan to reach a certain targeted (and hopefully niche) market that needs or desires your product or service, and then launch it to see if people will actually buy it. Using the aforementioned superficially catchy line insults everyone's intelligence, so please refrain. You either have customers that will buy your product or service and an actual business, or you have a charity, or a hobby. You may think your idea is so great that there just has to be a market out there that will buy it. Please stop the insanity and figure out who your customer really is.

Opinions of our friends, family, and ourselves ain't market research. Unless you are Steve Jobs (which you probably aren't), if you desire market research, please do more than ask your friends or family about your latest business idea. Now, if you have no desire to obtain market research and have a high risk tolerance for launching that business, then go right ahead. Some are successful at this model, but it is very rare. But don't complain that you lost money on a venture where you should've done more market research but chose to go the easy route by only seeking it from those who would most likely agree with your point of view. Beware asking a small circle of people for information on which your business fate hinges, since those closest to us will likely tell us what we want to hear.

Unless you are a personality or public figure (politician, musician, speaker, or radio/TV host), name your business something other than your name. This bothers me since it usually reflects ego and overconfidence in the owner's personal brand to grow and sustain the business. It is also usually indicative of a company that could be run much better. Most owners of smaller companies think that they *are* the company and that if they leave or die, it won't survive without them. The truth is, that the way they usually set things up, they are correct in that assessment. So please name your business something other than your name; that act should be a symbol of how the company has been built to succeed in future generations. Or if you really want to use your name, please use your last name only. We don't need another "The Suzy Smith Company."

Increasingly, the mass marketing is turning into a mass of niches.

Chris Anderson

Premium pricing to a niche market is usually better than competing on price in a commoditized market. The latter is a vicious race to the bottom, and in order to survive, you must have size and scale. Being forced to compete on price and steal your competitors' customers in order to gain market share is not the ideal way to work. Companies that carve out a niche market can dominate that space if they play their cards right. This is what W. Chan Kim and Renée Mauborgne talked about in their book *Blue Ocean Strategy*. They implore companies to find new markets they can dominate. What business wants to duke it out in fierce competition when they can focus on markets where they have little to no competition? Terry Kohler, a successful business leader and investor with whom I have had the pleasure of working, has a holding company called Windway Capital. His capital company owns a controlling interest in two such companies: North Sails and Vollrath. Each company generates over $300 million in annual revenues catering to highly specialized, niche markets where they dominate market share and have little in the way of competition. Vollrath has acquired over a dozen companies over the last forty years. I want to be a part of these types of organizations, and you should too.

And it is usually better to be second to market. True pioneers are rarely rewarded for their efforts. A lot of entrepreneurs dream of being the first to discover some new field or market. But the reality is that the people who get there first rarely have the best success. Just ask medical pioneers Barry Marshall and Robin Warren about how long they were ridiculed for their discovery that the H Pylori bacteria was the cause of some cases of gastritis and stomach ulcers. It took over twenty years for their work to be recognized with a Nobel Prize. Or question John Nash, the father of modern economic equilibrium/game theory, how long it was before his ideas were accepted and validated by his Nobel Prize . . . about forty years. And none of these men were able to significantly benefit financially from their work.

The sweet spot is to be second, third, or fourth to market, not first, but that is extremely hard to time properly. Apple wasn't first to market with a digital music player; neither was Microsoft Windows the first operating software. The company that quickly builds on the failures of the first-to-market company, learning from their mistakes and improving on their initial efforts, is likely to reap a majority of the market without having to invest the same R&D money. So see if you can take something from a first-to-market competitor, improve it inexpensively and meaningfully, and market it; you just might score a base hit or even a home run.

I have always believed that writing advertisements is the second most profitable form of writing. The first, of course, is ransom notes.

Philip Dusenberry

We often mess up our writing efforts in some form or another. Whether mixing metaphors, misusing idioms, or overusing exclamation points, all caps, or filler words, we are all guilty. Consider each of these the next time you write or speak something.

I think our use of mixed metaphors stems from the ADD/ADHD culture more and more of us have grown up in. We simply don't think through what we say or write before we say it, and something like the following comes out: "So now what we are dealing with is the rubber meeting the road, and instead of biting the bullet on these issues, we just want to punt." This is an actual quote from the *Chicago Tribune*, cited by *The New Yorker*, August 13, 2007. Here's another dandy from *The Wall Street Journal*, May 9, 1997: "A Pentagon staffer, complaining that efforts to reform the military have been too timid: 'It's just ham-fisted salami-slicing by the bean counters.'" And here's one more for good measure: "All at once he was alone in this noisy hive with no place to roost" (Tom Wolfe, *The Bonfire of the Vanities*). You get the picture; we need to slow down and think through what we are going to say or write before we let a metaphor fly out of our mouth. Others are paying attention, and using mixed metaphors lowers others' perception of us.

Please stop misusing and misspelling idioms. I know this might make me a grammar snob, but misused/misspelled idioms are too prevalent today and indicate the lack of proper education for many of us. Here are a few of the most common misspelled idioms:

1. It's "All intents and purposes" not "All intensive purposes"
2. "Dog eat dog world" not "Dog-e-dog" or "doggie dog"
3. "Wreaking havoc" not "Wrecking" or "reeking havoc"
4. "Free rein" not "Free reign"
5. "Sleight of hand" not "Slight of hand"
6. "Toe the line" not "tow the line"
7. "Whet your appetite" not "Wet your appetite"
8. "Lo and behold" not "Low and behold"
9. "Waiting with bated breath" not "Waiting with baited breath"
10. "Home in on" not "Hone in on"

Any copy that runs on a billboard should fit on the back of a business card.

John Pavao

Have you noticed how many billboards, yard signs, print advertising, web advertising, etc., have way too much text? And the font size is almost always too small to read at a distance? This drives me crazy. What do marketers think they are going to accomplish by bombarding the public with too much and too small text? They lack the discipline to use fewer words to say the same thing. It is easier to pack in more words to explain our point of view. We think more complexity will get someone's attention, but less is more. Just ask Apple; their products, packaging, and advertising are simple and uncluttered. Less text will allow for larger font and tighter focus on the text that is truly important.

Most of you know exactly what I mean when I say "Death by PowerPoint." People either read verbatim what they wrote on their slides, or they put too much text on each slide, making it hard to read or both. Or they have too many slides given the allotted speaking time. A good rule of thumb is Guy Kawasaki's 10/20/30 rule: Have no more than 10 slides, speak for no longer than 20 minutes, and use no font size smaller than 30 points. Also, know your audience, so you can adapt your PowerPoint presentation style to fit their needs. And please make your written PowerPoint bullet points as succinct as possible and expound upon them when you deliver your presentation. Remember, less is more, simpler is better, and shorter is superior. We will all thank you!

If advertising had a little more respect for the public, the public would have a lot more respect for advertising.

James Randolph Adams

Stop using so many exclamation points, repeated words, and ALL CAPS!!! You only serve to lessen the impact of your message by overusing them. Using one or two exclamation points at the end of a sentence is okay if you don't use them on every other sentence, or even every other paragraph for that matter. The same goes for ALL CAPS; please use them sparingly. Using both too frequently is like shouting all the time, and eventually we tune you out as either unprofessional or ignorant. And please refrain from uSiNg AlTeRnAtInG lower- and uppercase letters. Our eyes and minds will thank you. If you think this gimmick showcases your creativity, you are out of touch with reality.

Please don't repeat certain words excessively. (I will admit I am working on this myself.) Some irritating filler word examples for speeches are "um," "uh," "ah," "you know," "I think," "just," "like," "basically," "actually," "kinda," and "I dunno"; other filler words used in public prayers are "Father God," "Jesus," "Holy Spirit," and "Heavenly Father." We tend to use these as fillers to cover for lack of prepared thought and to avoid silence. These are not bad if used sparingly, but please severely limit them, slow down your thoughts, and speak more intentionally and deliberately. When we speak to someone in person, we don't keep repeating their name over and over during our conversation, so why keep repeating "God" during prayers? If we rely on filler in our public speaking, our listeners are left with the impression that we aren't smart, polished, or prepared. A way to break this habit is to become aware of how often it happens by recording a video of yourself speaking. You can also practice chunking your words. Chunking is the technique of grouping a few sentences together followed by a short pause, then grouping the next few sentences together followed by another pause, etc.

Closing Thoughts

The clock is running. Make the most of today. Time waits for no man. Yesterday is history. Tomorrow is a mystery. Today is a gift. That's why it is called the present.

Alice Morse Earle

Don't be discouraged by others' maturity. Start where you are today and grow from there. Yesterday is past, and nothing can change it, as much as we might want to. Do not be dispirited by your lack of growth compared to others; once you have admitted your shortcomings, develop habits that move you towards more maturity and selfless leadership. I don't condemn your past selfish behavior if you are genuinely trying to change it, and neither should you. We are all in this together, and we are all at different stages of maturation in our life. That doesn't make one person better than another. The fact that there are always others that are more self-sacrificing leaders than we are should incessantly drive us to be better, no matter what level we achieve.

Leadership shouldn't be a transfer of knowledge but should be knowledge applied and connected.

@RobPene

The picture I have painted of leadership in this book is not altogether a pretty one. Leadership is full of denials, dilemmas, frustrations, misadventures, and betrayals. It is not the path to universal respect and unlimited power that so many of us are looking for. In short, leadership sucks.

You may be wondering, "If this is true, then why should I want to be a leader?"

My first response to that is, "Well, maybe you shouldn't."

Far be it from me to dishearten any prospective leader (especially one who has done me the courtesy of reading my book). But bad leaders cause a lot of damage to the people they lead—and to themselves. Not everyone who wants to be a leader is ready to lead. We would all be better off if prospective leaders took a cold hard look at what it will cost. What is the nature of this role you seek to fill? What will you have to give up in order to do it well? Are you ready to pay that price? If this book has opened your eyes to the costs of leadership, then it has accomplished at least one of its purposes.

But there is encouragement in this picture of leadership as well—the best encouragement a leader could receive. Rather than offering you the momentary and hollow satisfactions of selfish "leadership," servant leadership produces lasting and fulfilling results. It generates a legacy of improved lives, healthy relationships—even treasure in heaven.

I don't know if you buy that last point, but in my mind, it's the key to the whole puzzle of how to lead in a life-giving way. I believe that selfless service is the right thing to do, but—you may have noticed this—few of us have the willpower to do the right thing for its own sake. For me, whatever power I have to serve selflessly comes not from within me but from following Jesus Christ. He is the definition of servant leadership; if you want to know what it really looks like, try reading the story of Him in the four Gospels (I recommend starting with the Gospel of John). I believe that by uniting our lives with His, following His teaching and example, we can become more like Him and greater participants in eternal joy. If you'd like to know more about how to follow Christ, connect with me on Twitter or LinkedIn.

This book cannot attempt to cover all the ways in which servant leadership is enacted in everyday life. I intend it to merely serve as a guide to learn and put it into practice several concrete leadership principles. We all can read many books on a variety of subjects, but until we practice the concepts in them, we have learned nothing other than "head knowledge." And while the sheer volume of leadership ideas may seem overwhelming, don't be discouraged or complacent. Simply practice one concept per day or per week until it becomes a habit; then move on to the next thing. The practice is hard, but the proficiency is worth it.

Leadership Books I Recommend

- *The One Minute Manager* by Kenneth Blanchard
- *Go Put Your Strengths to Work* by Marcus Buckingham
- *Good to Great* by Jim Collins
- *The Seven Habits of Highly Effective People* by Stephen R. Covey
- Any of Peter Drucker's books
- *The Top Ten Mistakes Leaders Make* by Hans Finzel
- *The E-Myth* by Michael E. Gerber
- *Servant Leadership* by Robert K. Greenleaf
- *The Servant* by James C. Hunter
- *Leadership and Crisis* by Bobby Jindal
- *The Case for Servant Leadership* by Dr. Kent M. Keith
- *The Five Dysfunctions of a Team* by Patrick Lencioni
- Any of John Maxwell's books
- *Wooden on Leadership* by John Wooden

My Current and Forthcoming Books and Resources

Why Leadership Sucks Online Video Course

Currently available at Udemy.com

Miles and Christopher Paul Elliott will guide your leadership journey to increase leadership IQ and enhance effectiveness using real-world examples. Chris is a servant leadership speaker and author of *Thought Shredder*. Video sessions include: Self-Awareness, First Impressions Are Lasting Impressions... As Long As You Let Them Last, and Are you a Micromanager or a Macromanager?

If you enjoyed either volume one or two of the Why Leadership Sucks books, plug into these thirty-three lectures with a full ninety minutes of video packed with actionable insights, bonus MP3s, PowerPoints, and other resources.

Why Career Advice Sucks: Join Generation Flux and Build an Agile, Adaptable, and Resilient Career

Currently available online in ebook, paperback, and audio book formats

"The illiterate of the 21st century will not be those who cannot read or write, but those who cannot learn, unlearn, and relearn."

(Futurist Alvin Toffler)

The new currency of a successful career is to find a niche where we bring value that not many others can. No longer is a good work ethic enough to secure and retain a job with middle-class pay and benefits as it was a generation ago. My book, *Why Career Advice Sucks: Join Generation Flux and Build an Agile, Adaptable, and Resilient Career*, addresses this change in employment and how to navigate the new work environment.

The Serial Specialist: Who They Are and Why You MUST Hire Them to Thrive

"The division of labour offers us the first example of how, as long as man remains in natural society, that is as long as a cleavage exists between the particular and the common interest, as long therefore as activity is not voluntarily, but naturally, divided, man's own deed becomes an alien power opposed to him, which enslaves him instead of being controlled by him. For as soon as labour is distributed, each man has a particular, exclusive sphere of activity, which is forced upon him and from which he cannot escape."

(SOCIALIST KARL MARX)

"Specialization may be all well very well if you happen to have skills particularly suited to these jobs, or if you are passionate about a niche area of work, and of course there is also the benefit of feeling pride in being considered an expert. But there is equally the danger of becoming dissatisfied by the repetition inherent in many specialist professions...

"Moreover, our culture of specialization conflicts with something most of us intuitively recognize, but which career advisers are only beginning to understand: we each have multiple selves... We have complex, multi-faceted experiences, interests, values and talents, which might mean that we could also find fulfillment as a web designer, or a community police officer, or running an organic cafe.

"This is a potentially liberating idea with radical implications. It raises the possibility that we might discover career fulfillment by escaping the confines of specialization and cultivating ourselves as wide achievers ... allowing the various petals of our identity to fully unfold."

(PHILOSOPHER ROMAN KRZNARIC)

Do you hire specialists in your specific industry but continually feel disappointed with their innovation and creativity levels? Are you routinely rejecting generalists for fear of them not sticking around very long? Or are you frustrated with your own career, sensing a kind of indentured servitude to your particular work specialty? Do you yearn to do other things? Do you get bored after a few years in one type of work?

If so, *The Serial Specialist* is for you. Miles will help you understand why these outliers are typically outcasts but should be brought into your corporate fold to achieve success in this challenging economy. You will learn why you and they are to be highly valued, and how to identify, hire, and retain adaptable, agile, and innovative talent.

Coming soon

The Opportunity Cost of Christ

"We drive our cars 60-70 miles per hour with an oncoming car doing the same with only a white line and six to eight feet separating us. We place our faith that every car will not cross into our lane. We fly on airplanes that take us over oceans, trusting the pilots with our very lives. We ride on thrilling amusement rides that take us several stories into the air and travel fifty to seventy miles per hour down a winding slope. We trust the operators of that ride with our own mortality.

"There is a great irony in the fact that we can place our faith in such things but cannot place our faith in the hands of our Creator."

(OS HILLMAN, TAKEN FROM MARKETPLACE-LEADERS.ORG)

We all have faith and trust in many features of modern life, seeking the allusion of security. Among them are a paper money system, accumulated wealth, relationships, food, alcohol, government, business, and education. We even believe that the brakes on our cars will stop us and that doctors will heal our ailments. So why do we have such a hard time putting our faith and trust in Christ?

My forthcoming book, *The Opportunity Cost of Christ*, argues that trusting in and following Christ is not a leap of faith in defiance of reason, but the reasonable conclusion of a rational mind.

Coming soon

About the Author

Miles Anthony Smith, an ambivert and serial specialist, has held senior, executive leadership positions for businesses and non-profits over the past fifteen years. He has broad management skills across many functional business disciplines in accounting, finance, human resources, marketing, and leadership, earning a Bachelor of Music Composition degree from Oral Roberts University and a master's in Business Administration from Oklahoma State University. Miles currently works for Imaginasicom as director of digital marketing. Miles is the author of the *Why Leadership Sucks* and the *Why Career Advice Sucks* series.

Born a Hoosier, raised an Okie, and currently residing in the frozen tundra of Green Bay, Wisconsin, Miles is happily married to Carolyn and is a proud father of three. Now in his mid-thirties, he was fortunate to have been given a significant leadership opportunity by his father at the age of twenty-five. He is a classically trained violist, violinist, and composer, with passions in the fields of small-business management, marketing, macroeconomics, servant leadership, and classical education.

Miles, a Generation X leader and author, cares enough about organizational health to make the tough decisions, hire and coach the right people, set clear expectations, develop a strong team culture, and strengthen organizational cash flow, exhibiting both humility and fierce resolve. His mission in life is: "To chart the course, pave the pathway, and light the lane for others to eclipse my own success in leadership."

Notes

1. HT Andy Stanley
2. HT John Maxwell
3. For those of you who have no idea who I am talking about, check him out on YouTube: http://youtu.be/KQDNofmfCFQ
4. Don't you think? Now that it's in your head, you might as well listen to the whole song: http://www.youtube.com/watch?v=Jne9t8sHpUc.
5. See http://en.wikipedia.org/wiki/Body_language
6. http://phobos.apple.com/WebObjects/MZStore.woa/wa/viewPodcast?id=290055666
7. For those who don't know what a mini-me is, please refer to this clip from the Austin Powers trilogy of movies: http://youtu.be/tkmi_UTsjtE
8. Another hat tip to Andy Stanley on this one; check out the monthly *Andy Stanley Leadership Podcast* on iTunes: http://phobos.apple.com/WebObjects/MZStore.woa/wa/viewPodcast?id=290055666.
9. http://www.familybusinessinstitute.com/index.php/Succession-Planning
10. There are tons of academic research to support this principle. If you want to read more about it, feel free to contact Dr. Basu.
11. http://en.wikipedia.org/wiki/Perfect_information
12. Thanks Dr. Hatley!
13. Ecclesiastes 3:1, ESV
14. HT Dave Ramsey
15. My favorite economist is John Mauldin. Much of what I write in the next several pages I owe to him.
16. http://www.investopedia.com/terms/a/arbitrage.asp
17. blueharborresort.com

54491829R00126

Made in the USA
Columbia, SC
01 April 2019